SLAND SH

reet ir

# THE DESERTER'S TALE

Joshua Key enlisted in the US Armed Forces
in 2002 to lift his family out of poverty. In early
2003, Key was sent to Iraq. This is his story.

Lawrence Hill is an award-winning Canadian
novelist and journalist.

# THE DESERTER'S TALE

## WHY I WALKED AWAY FROM THE WAR IN IRAQ

JOSHUA KEY

*as told to Lawrence Hill*

TEXT PUBLISHING MELBOURNE AUSTRALIA

The Text Publishing Company
Swann House
22 William Street
Melbourne Victoria 3000
Australia
www.textpublishing.com.au

First published in the US by Grove Atlantic 2007
This edition published by Text Publishing 2007

Design by Chong
Typeset by J & M Typesetting
Printed by Griffin Press

National Library of Australia
Cataloguing-in-Publication data:

Key, Joshua.
The deserter's tale : why I walked away from the war in Iraq.

ISBN 978-1-921145-90-2.

1. Key, Joshua. 2. Iraq War, 2003- - Personal narratives, American.
3. Iraq War, 2003- - Desertions - United States. 4. Military deserters -
United States - Biography. 5. Americans - Canada. I. Hill, Lawrence.
II. Title.

956.70443

*I dedicate this book to my wife, Brandi Key, and to our children, Zackary, Adam, Philip and Anna. I wouldn't have made it this far without them.*

JOSHUA KEY

# CONTENTS

# PROLOGUE

I never thought I would lose my country, and never dreamed that it would lose me. I was raised as a patriotic American, taught to respect my government and to believe in my president.

Just a decade ago, I was playing high school football, living in a trailer with my mom and stepdad, working at Kentucky Fried Chicken and hoping to raise a family one day in the only town I knew: Guthrie, Oklahoma, population 10,000. Back then, I would have laughed out loud if somebody had predicted that I would become a wanted criminal, live as a fugitive in my own country and turn my own wife and children into refugees as I fled with them across the border.

Before I could survive and escape the war in Iraq, I had to survive my own childhood. I shot a .357 magnum on my ninth birthday, brought down my first deer by the age of twelve, and could clean, load and shoot any of dozens of firearms that my stepfather kept in our trailer. I was an excellent shot before I was old enough to shave. I drank alcohol of every kind, trashed two cars on country roads and fought anybody who was willing.

But even in my earliest years, I knew right from wrong. It wasn't right to kill puppies with a hammer, which is why I shot and buried a litter of pups before my grandfather could get at them in his old-fashioned way. Iraq took all of the fun out of guns, for me, but even in the days that I still loved shooting, I stopped hunting after dropping a deer with a four-inch bullet through the neck.

Even though I was taught that it was shameful to get licked in a fight and come home beaten, I knew that it wasn't right to gang up on someone, pick on a smaller person or to keep on punching after your opponent had fallen. I knew it was wrong to attack any person who was weak or defenceless, and everything about my early years at home reinforced that belief.

I was born in 1978, and we didn't have books or newspapers at home. I had heard of the Vietnam War, but didn't know when or why Americans had fought in it. But I can guarantee you this: if any man had told me that he had deserted our army in wartime, I would have called him a coward right to his face. There were just some things you didn't do. By the time I was in high school, I felt that it would be an honour to serve my country at war, and even to die for it. I couldn't imagine any circumstances in which an American soldier would walk away from his own armed forces and thus betray his country.

Looking back, I would say that many parts of my life in Oklahoma prepared me for the war in Iraq. Our two-bedroom trailer baked in the Oklahoma sun and froze in the winter, so I was as ready for extreme weather as any American. Growing up on my grandfather's forty-acre farm, I learned to fix just about anything that was broken and make pretty well anything run. I was only a private first class when I went to war, but at least I had farmboy skills, and my officers came to count on them. I was the one they came to, over and over again, to connect air-conditioners to generators, hot-wire trucks, run our own wires to Iraqi electricity lines and assemble plastic explosives.

As a child, I watched many times as J. W. Barker—my third and final stepfather—drank himself into a stupor and beat up my mother. I grew up learning to expect abuse. J. W. loved to bring over his drinking buddies and have them watch while I worked with his guns. I used to bet them about whether I could hit a small target with a .22 rifle. While they tipped back beer, I would hang a string from a tree, pull it taut by tying it to an old fire extinguisher on the ground, stand back fifty paces and blast through the target nearly every time. At $10 a pop, it was the fastest pocket money I ever earned. I earned a good bit of it. Growing up, I shot beer bottles, Coke cans, hanging string and snakes; I was a fine marksman before joining the army.

But the preparation for Iraq was more than physical. Growing up poor in Oklahoma also prepared me mentally. It was as if my mind was a little garden, with the days of my young life planting seeds of war.

I lived with my mother, brother, father and then a variety of stepdads on the farm of my grandfather, Elmer Porter. I often ate at his table when there was no food at home, or when my mother was too depressed to get out of bed. Elmer had fought in the Korean War and then worked for years at the Tinker Air Force Base in Oklahoma City. Five other living relatives had served in the US military or gone to war. I didn't think much about war, but I had no objection to it.

One time a teacher in Guthrie got a worried look in her eye, put her hand on my arm and asked, 'Is everything all right at home?'

'Yes ma'am,' I told her, 'it's just fine thank you.' And I thought it was true. I knew plenty of people who lived harder lives than me. One friend had parents who both ran away from home, leaving him behind to fend for himself.

School was not exactly my strong point. Nobody in my immediate family had gone beyond high school, and I didn't see the point of further studies. I had one cousin who went to college four years, and the only job he could get in Oklahoma City was managing a waffle house. Seemed like a waste of time and money to me. I didn't read in school and hated to write, but I did enjoy math.

I didn't yet know what lay in my future, but one set of strangers already did. Before I had even graduated from high school, a string of army recruiters started showing up at our trailer, banging on the flimsy door that blew open on windy nights, promising health insurance and higher education in exchange for military service. They were smart men, those recruiters. They didn't waste time at the doors of doctors and lawyers, but came straight for me. The recruiters said I could even join the army at the age of seventeen, with my mother's signature. She chased them off the property, but the damage was already done. The recruiters had planted the seed. They didn't get me for another few years, but they had made me aware that if I ever got tired of the minimum wage, there was always the adventure of life in the army.

But back in high school, I didn't think about joining the army, and I didn't plan on going to war. Guthrie was all that I knew and all I imagined, and the things I wanted then are the things I want now: a few acres of land for the kids to play on, with maybe a horse or two, a few pigs and a mess of chickens in a coop.

Since I was a boy, I have known that I wanted to make my living as a welder. There's something about welding that I loved from the first time that J. W. showed me how to turn on a torch. Under your flame, the metal flows like lava. You follow its movement and work with its nature. Sometimes you mess up, but that's okay. When things go wrong, all you have to do is melt down the metal and start all over again. Nobody minds. Nobody's hurt. You fix your mistakes and get it right the next time, working the lava so that things stay together. The freedom to say 'No that's not good enough, let me try again' is what I love about welding.

To this day, there is no work I'd rather do than hold a welding torch. If I had my druthers, I'd move away with Brandi and our four children and get myself enrolled in the welding program at the College of the North Atlantic in Newfoundland. I've been hearing about the school for years. They say it's one of the best on the continent. But I wouldn't be ready for welding, quite yet.

I still get blackouts. I still wake up screaming in the middle of the night. I take pills to keep the nightmares at bay. The dreams are like sleeping dogs, and sometimes they haunt me during the day. Recently, I was driving on a country road and saw a cardboard box on the shoulder. Only I didn't think *cardboard box*. I thought it was a bomb, planted just for me, like all the explosives I set off in Iraq and that it had been placed there for me and my fellow soldiers. I swerved wildly onto the grass by the side of the road, to get out of its kill zone, to escape the shrapnel. When I came to, I was sweating and shaking behind the steering wheel.

I have never hit my wife or my children or anyone else during my blackouts, but I have been known to throw things and to rip light fixtures from ceilings. I have been known to shout words of mayhem and war, but I never remember these things when I finally come to in Brandi's arms.

The doctors call it Post-traumatic Stress Disorder. They say I'll have it for life, and just have to learn to deal with it.

I can only imagine what would have happened if I had not deserted the American army in Iraq. I guess it's not that hard to tell. There are only a few options. If I had gone back to war, I could have been taken out by a bullet, or mortars, or a rocket-propelled grenade. I could have been forced to kill an innocent person, or more than one.

I can say with relief and gratitude that I have never killed anybody, Iraqi or American. I have enough troubles as it is living with my own demons, and I'm not sure how I would have kept going with innocent blood on my hands. But I know there is a chance that if I had killed someone else, I would have gone on later to kill myself.

If I had returned to duty after a two-week vacation with my family, I would have had to go on raiding, arresting and intimidating people who were like me in the most surprising ways. They were poor, with almost no way to escape their miserable situations. They were hungry, but they were amazingly resourceful. I'll never forget the image of an Iraqi man driving up to a traffic checkpoint where I stood with my weapon at the ready. The gas line in his car had been ruptured. Outside the window, he was holding up a gallon of gas, so it could flow down through a rubber hose to the engine as he inched forward in the car. He was an ordinary man, using all of his ingenuity to survive in extraordinary circumstances.

I was stationed in Fort Carson, Colorado, when President George W. Bush declared war on Iraq, and within two weeks

I was flying into a war zone. I wasn't happy about it, but I went willingly. I believed what my president and my commanders had told me. Somebody had to rid the world of weapons of mass destruction. Somebody had to depose the evil tyrant Saddam Hussein. Somebody had to make the world safe from terrorists, who had overtaken Iraq and were threatening our lives. I felt it was better for me to help do the job now, than leave it to my own children. Even Brandi, who was left alone at home with Zachary, Adam and Philip, said to me: 'You get 'em, Josh, before they get you. Even if it's a kid. They're terrorists too.' I believed her. I felt the same way.

In all the military training I had received in Missouri and Colorado, Iraqis were never called people, or citizens, or men, women and children. They were called 'sand niggers', 'rag heads', 'habbibs', 'hajjis' and, most of all, 'terrorists'. In the army of the United States of America, those were our only words for them. My superiors made no distinction between civilians and combatants. As far as they were concerned—and I came to believe them entirely on this point—there were only enemies in Iraq, and all Iraqis were enemies.

I know that many Americans have their minds made up about people like me. They think we are cowards who just couldn't take it. I don't blame them. I had my own mind made up about war deserters, long before I set foot in Iraq. But I know right from wrong. I had a conscience by the age of six. I had to suspend it for a while, in Iraq. Soldiers are taught: Army First, God Second, Family Third. I am not a coward, and I never flinched from danger. The easiest thing would have been to keep on doing what they were telling me to do. Ever so slowly, as the jets raced and the illumination rounds burned and the houses fell during the long Iraqi nights, my conscience returned. It could no longer be Army First, God Second and Family Third. It had to be the tiny voice inside me that would not sleep any longer. *I am not this man*, I told myself. *I cannot do these things any longer.*

This is the story of how that voice finally grew louder than the rumbling of tanks and the blaze of gunfire and the hollering of commanders. This is the story of how it came to be that I went to Iraq as a private first class in the United States army. This is the story of what I did to the Iraqi people and what I saw other Americans do to them, and why I deserted the war and became an outlaw in my own country. I was made to be a criminal in Iraq, but I am a criminal no longer, and I am never going back.

# ONE

# CHILDHOOD

I could have used a father's advice before deciding to join the army. A father could have guided me through my worst hours in Iraq. And by the time I ran away from the American army, I was starving for the counsel of an older man. I wished for a father with two basic qualities: knowledge of war and love of his son. But there was no such man in my life. There was no one at all who fit the bill. Anonymously, I called an army lawyer. His job was to advise soldiers in distress, but the only thing he gave me was an earful. 'Soldier,' he said on the phone, 'you've got two choices. You get back to Iraq, or you go to jail.'

Hanging up, I took comfort in the arms of my wife. Without Brandi, I could never have made it through the hell of living as a fugitive. I was a total mess. I couldn't sleep. Couldn't handle crowds. Couldn't even stand in a supermarket checkout line. All around me, I imagined grenades launching, bullets pinging off concrete and the heads of decapitated Iraqis accusing me of war crimes. I kept reaching for my weapon—an M-249 squad automatic weapon, thirty-six pounds fully loaded—and felt naked without it.

In Iraq I learned that every soldier has his story. One man who was ripped apart by an explosion in his tank told me as I picked up his leg and put it beside him on the stretcher, 'Now I get to see my daughter.' Others sank under the weight of 'Dear John' letters and had no reason at all to go home.

As for my own story, I am not yet thirty but feel as if I have already lived four distinct lives. In my first life, I lived at home in Guthrie, Oklahoma, and then started a family of my own with Brandi. In the second life, I spent eighteen months in military training and at war in Iraq. In the third life, I deserted the American army and hid in Philadelphia for fourteen months, slinking from one cheap hotel to the next under the cover of darkness. In this current life, I am hanging on in a new land with my wife and children, waiting to see if the Canadian government will let us stay.

I grew up on a farm on the outskirts of Guthrie, a small town north of Oklahoma City. The land was owned by my grandfather, Elmer Porter, who bought it after serving in the Korean War. Elmer had been an airplane mechanic at Tinker Air Force Base, but he was retired by the time I came along. He lived on the property with my grandmother, Doris. Some aunts, uncles and cousins of mine had their own houses on the property, and my mother, brother and I lived in a two-bedroom trailer about 200 yards from my grandparents' house. Before heading to school, I would often stop by my grandparents' for breakfast. Doris always made me eggs over easy, and Elmer cooked bacon in an iron skillet. My memories of eating with them are the fondest of my childhood. They were the rocks in my life, and I took refuge in their home when it was too hot or too violent in the trailer.

Doris and Elmer were Pentecostal Christians. Elmer said it was wrong for a man to hit his wife. I never saw him raise a finger against anyone. He showed me how to whittle and taught me how to fix motors, pumps and fences on the farm. He kept ten ancient tractors that he couldn't bear to part with. Every spring, while I held his tools, he would tune them all up and drive each one around the property.

When I was thirteen or so, my grandfather said there was no room on the farm for seven new puppies. He had a quick death in mind. It was nothing to him—nothing more than avoiding a situation where he would have to feed too many dogs. I knew he didn't mean to be cruel, and I suspect he thought that with his sharp blows to the head, he was bringing them an instant and painless death. But I had seen his solution before and just couldn't stand by and watch him take a hammer and kill the puppies that way again. So I dug one big hole in the woods behind my trailer, spread the puppies out in the ground, aimed my .22 rifle and shot them each once quickly at point-blank range, hoping to spare them the misery of my grandfather's hammer. I covered the pups with dirt, stood up with the shovel, took a step back and could hear two of them still weeping under the ground. I dug them up in a panic. Two of them were barely moving, but they were still whimpering. I knew they were suffering and I didn't like to see anything suffer. I choked back the realisation that I had just caused them more pain than my grandfather would have with his own technique. I ran back to the trailer as fast as I could, opened the unlocked gun cabinet, and scoured the shelves for a weapon that I knew would be loaded and much more powerful. I grabbed a silver, nine-millimetre Rugger pistol and ran back to the hole. I shot every round from the gun—I believe it was thirteen bullets—into the bodies below. My lungs were heaving, and my body was wracked with sobs, and I shot indiscriminately until I knew for sure that all the puppies were dead. I didn't speak to a single person about what I had done, and for weeks I was haunted by the killing of the weeping dogs.

My grandmother Doris smoked Virginia Slims and was always crocheting, sewing or knitting. She watched 'Walker, Texas Ranger' every day on TV. She used to make pecan pies and let me eat them warm. On the nights that it wasn't safe in the trailer, I slept near my grandmother in her bedroom. Doris was religious but she swore like a trooper. She was reliable on one hand and easygoing on the other, and I loved my grandmother more than anyone else in the world.

The day before I flew from Fort Carson to Kuwait, I called Doris on the telephone. I told her that I would think of her every day while I was overseas, and asked what she was doing that day.

'I'm covering all the house windows with plastic,' she said.

I chuckled. 'Grandma, what's all that foolishness about?'

'In case of chemical attack,' she said. 'Half the folks in Guthrie are doing the same thing. People say we might get chemical attacked, so they're covering up their windows.'

I laughed out loud. I wished I could be there to hug the woman and fix her a glass of iced tea.

'Grandma, you ought to sit down and relax. Forget covering the windows. Plastic won't help you if we get chemical-attacked. If that happens, you might as well just bend over and kiss your ass goodbye because we're all gonna die.'

She laughed and said it was probably true. She said that I should take good care of myself, and that she would always love me. I never heard her voice again. Doris died seventeen days after I flew into war.

■

When I was still a teenager, my father almost came back for me. His name was Donald Ernest Key. I knew little about him. He had three sons from an earlier marriage but I've only met them once. He was a welder and he drank too much. He took off when I was three and never paid my mother a cent of child support or alimony. The next time I saw him was twelve years later, when he was lying in his own casket. I heard that he had died in an accident while working on an oil rig off the coast of Africa.

I was told not to go to his funeral, because he had remarried and his relatives might think I was chasing his money. So I didn't go to the funeral, but I went to the visitation. I spoke with his sister, who said she had heard that Dad had come to see me recently. That seemed a strange thing to say, since I had never seen or heard from him.

A little later, I wandered through the woods on our property and came across a beaten-up old lawn chair in a grove of trees. Empty liquor bottles were strewn around the chair. Peering through the growth, I could see my own yard. I assumed that my father had hidden there to watch me coming and going on school days. Who else would have been hiding in the woods on our family farm, twenty miles south of Guthrie, emptying bottle after bottle of Wild Turkey? It sure wasn't my stepfather, J. W. Barker, who kept his own beer locked up in a refrigerator in his bedroom. My father was said to be a fine welder, but he never found the courage to speak to me.

My mother's name is Judy Porter. She is fifty, and she lives in Guthrie. She has heart troubles and a pacemaker and uses an oxygen tank to breathe. I speak to her almost every day by telephone, but haven't been able to see her since I went AWOL four years ago. Most deserters get caught, and they get caught by being stupid. They just can't resist the urge to visit their loved ones. It was fortunate that Brandi and the children came with me the moment I went into hiding. And it was a good thing I never went back to see my mother. The military police would have caught me for sure. Mom told me that after my desertion she saw strange cars parked down the road. Even Captain Bower, my commanding officer in Iraq, called my mother on the telephone. Bower told her that a number of soldiers had deserted his company of 120 men, and that he had caught every last one of them except for me. He warned that she could be charged if she helped me in any way. 'Aiding and abetting a criminal is against the law', is the way Mom said he put it.

I avoided detection by following every word of training that I received in the army. When your job is to defuse land-mines and to set plastic explosives on people's doors before busting into their homes, you either pay attention to details or you die with your head up your ass. After I went AWOL, there was one detail I never forgot. *If you don't want to get caught, don't go see your mother.*

Unlike the men who walked in and out of my life, my mother did not have a drinking problem. However, by the time I was in high school, she rarely got out of bed or left the house. She never went to meet my teachers. She never drove to a football game to cheer me on. She hardly went anywhere at all. Looking back, I think she was depressed because she had married a string of alcoholics. Earlier, when she was healthier, she served coffee and meals at a local truck stop on the road to Oklahoma City. When I was nine, a trucker named James Willard Barker moved in with my mother and became my third stepdad. He stayed eleven years with my mother before he finally left.

I can credit J. W. with one thing. He did such awful things to my mother that I learned the hard way how not to act. Nobody deserves the kind of treatment that he dished out. J. W. intimidated and dominated my mother, younger brother and me. His reign of terror lasted until two things happened around the same time: I finally outgrew him, and he developed cirrhosis of the liver.

When I was a young boy, I doted for years on a black, brown and white 'weenie' dog with a ridiculously long tail. His name was Buttercup, and he slept in my bedroom. Not long after J. W. moved in, he made me put Buttercup outside on a freezing winter's night. I begged my Mom to let me bring Buttercup back in, but she said that I had to obey my stepfather. The next day, I searched everywhere for my dachshund. Two days later, I found Buttercup huddled under the trailer, frozen to death.

J. W. got rid of my mother's animals too. She had been keeping horses, goats and chickens for years, but J. W. sold every one of them off. Drinking money, I supposed.

It didn't take long before I hated the man and wished him dead. A short, muscular man who wore a cowboy hat and cowboy boots, J. W. kept dozens of loaded weapons in unlocked cases in the trailer. I learned how to use them all.

On my ninth birthday, as a lark while his drinking buddies looked on, J. W. let me hold his nickel-plated .357 magnum pistol.

'Go ahead,' he said, 'see how it feels. Pull the trigger—it's not loaded.'

When I pulled the trigger, a bullet exploded from the barrel. The gun flew up and rocked my shoulder, nearly knocking me over. Witnessing my humiliation, J. W. and his buddies bent over in laughter.

I already knew how to shoot a .22 rifle before J. W. came into my life, but under his watch I learned to clean, load and shoot every weapon in his collection. In the field behind our trailer, I shot pistols, shotguns and rifles. By the age of twelve, I was shooting M-14 and AK-47 assault rifles.

Someone gave me an Uzi around that time, and I used it to shoot snapping turtles in the pond near our farm. When I hit them, the turtles would fly up in the air and land on their backs in the water. I had a mortal fear of snakes, and one day spotted a large one wrapped around a tree. I ran home, loaded a twelve-gauge pump-action shotgun, raced back to the tree and blasted the sucker over and over. My grandfather, who had seen me while working outside, teased me about it for a long time. 'Did you need all those rounds for just one snake?' he asked.

I began to hunt at the age of nine or ten. I didn't need a permit because I was under age. A few years later on a hunting trip, I spotted a deer two hundred yards away. Aiming a

Remington 7-millimetre rifle with a scope, I shot a four-inch bullet into its neck. I felt a rush of adrenaline. But when I ran up to take a closer look, I found blood everywhere. It was shocking to me. I felt horrible. The animal seemed big-eyed and defenceless, its life utterly wasted. J. W. made me help as he hung the deer from a branch and gutted it. Blood and guts spilled over our hands and arms, but we had to keep moving so the meat wouldn't spoil. It didn't matter that we ate the meat, or that it tasted good. My first deer became my last, and I did not go hunting again.

J. W. was obsessed about guns, but everybody else in the family had them too. My mother kept one by the side of her bed, and to this day my eighty-year-old grandfather packs a pistol in his pocket.

Twice in my thirteenth year, I nearly shot J. W.

The first time, J. W. gave me a .410 shotgun and told me to put it away in the gun cabinet. To check if it was loaded, I pointed it at the window and pulled the trigger. When the shotgun blasted, most of the pellets hit the fireplace rather than out through the window. I missed J. W. by about an inch. He screamed and hollered about how I was a fat, stupid, dumb-assed retard.

The second time, I heard our trailer door open in the middle of the night. I reached for my .20 gauge shotgun, which I kept with rounds of ammunition in the bedroom that I shared with my brother, Tyler. I picked up the gun and stepped out into the hall, pointing it forward. At the same moment, J. W. stepped out with his AK-47 pointed at me.

The door had merely blown open in the wind. We saw each other just in time, lowered our weapons and returned to our bedrooms.

Gun accidents weren't uncommon in my world. J. W. had a daughter from a previous marriage, and she had a son named Nathan. For his fourteenth birthday, Nathan received a handgun from J. W. Later, Nathan played with it in his bedroom. While looking at the barrel, he pulled the trigger and blew his own head off. Everybody said it was an accident. And in high school I had a seventeen-year-old friend named Chris Coleman who died at a party when someone put a 9-millimetre pistol to his head and pulled the trigger. Then, too, the kids at the party assumed it was not loaded.

■

J. W. bossed me around and called me stupid and fat all the time, but he reserved the very worst for my mother. When J. W. got drunk, something evil came over him and he went looking for her.

Once, Mom got up from the dinner table and opened the dishwasher to reach for a plate. Without provocation, J. W. swept up behind her, grabbed the dishwasher door and slammed it shut against her hand. Mom let out a scream and went to hide in her room. She never wanted us to see her when she was in pain. Mom went to the doctor a few days later, claimed she had fallen down some stairs and came home in a cast. I wished that the doctor had paid a house call. He would have seen that there were no stairs in our trailer.

Maybe he would have demanded another explanation for the broken hand.

Another time, J. W. loaded Tyler and me into his car and raced up to the highway restaurant where Mom was working. As soon as he barged through the door, he began shouting that Mom had been sleeping with other men.

Mom stared at him, eyes wide. 'Are you crazy?' she said. 'Go away. I'm working.' But J. W. would not stop shouting.

Finally, the boss came out and told my mom to leave. She lost her job. Mom drove back home in another car, and I rode with her while she cried and said she had no idea what he had been talking about. I remember seeing him punch her when we got back home. After that, my mother stayed in bed most of the time, depressed and unable to do anything, for herself or for us.

I wasn't yet eleven.

Not long after Mom lost her job, the troubles continued. Alone in our bedroom, Tyler and I could feel the trailer shaking. We knew it was Mom, being thrown against the walls. I looked out through a crack in the door and saw J. W. rip a phone off the wall and use it to smash my mother in the head. As blood ran from her ear, I came out of my room. J. W. hollered at me to get back and to close the door behind me. Mom, too, pleaded with me to stay out of it. She went to the hospital and came home with a bandage like a turban around her head. J. W. had broken her eardrum.

Sometimes in the morning I would notice a scratch or a bruise on J. W.'s face. That would make me light up in a moment of private victory. The battle scars meant that my mother had managed to scratch or punch back at least once during the beating. I couldn't understand why she wouldn't leave him, and I couldn't believe that his brothers would just sit around and drink beer without a word of protest when J. W. beat my mother in front of them.

I wonder if seeing my mother get beaten up so many times led me to feel, in the end, that it was only normal that I, too, should have a few knocks in life.

When I was sixteen, I began my first part-time job. I worked at the Kentucky Fried Chicken outlet in Guthrie a few evenings a week, for about $5 an hour. One day, while I was changing an oil filter on a deep fryer, I accidentally touched vegetable oil that was boiling in a vat. The grease exploded against my face and one hand. I jumped back and leaned over a sink to throw water over my face and hand. I could feel that I had been seriously burned, so I asked the manager to call an ambulance. She was busy serving customers and refused to help me. I ran out the back door to my truck, to drive myself to the hospital. The truck had a flat. With blistering hands and a face that felt like it was on fire, I had to change the flat tyre before I could jump behind the steering wheel and drive with my third-degree burns to the hospital.

I never returned to work at Kentucky Fried Chicken, but I didn't stop to think that I deserved better treatment, and never even thought about making a complaint.

Somehow, I survived my childhood. Perhaps it helped to

feel normal and to know that other people had it much worse. Maybe they didn't have enough food to eat. Maybe their loved ones were sitting in prison. Maybe a man named Timothy McVeigh had just blown up their folks in Oklahoma City. It was probably just as well that I didn't know that my own life was difficult.

I wouldn't wish my own childhood on anyone, and I want to protect my own children from a life like my own. But I will say one thing for it. Learning to cope day after day with harshness gave me the strength to push through the nightmare in Iraq and the stubbornness to find a way out. Perhaps my childhood experiences made it possible for me to do the one thing that a soldier must never do: to think for myself and to question my commanders.

Oklahoma summers were hotter than hell. My brother and cousins and I would make mud pies and watch them dry out in the sun. It never took long, in 115-degree heat. My cousins liked to swim in the pond, but I stayed mostly out of the water because I lived in fear of cottonmouth snakes. We dug pretend war tunnels underground and shot paintballs at each other until, at thirteen, we graduated to whiskey and beer and racing down country roads in pick-up trucks.

We called the spring 'beer-drinking weather', and soon found two new ways to amuse ourselves. After drinking late into the night, we would go out cow-tipping in farmers' fields. Cows fall asleep on their feet, standing straight up, and we would sneak up and knock them over real fast. They had no balance at all, and would topple like bowling pins. Farmers didn't like our pranks, and we had to clear out as fast as we could before someone caught sight of our licence plates.

Our second amusement was mailbox crashing. A friend and I would go tearing down the road in my 1992 Nissan pick-up. While he drove, I leaned out the side window with a baseball bat, swinging at the country mailboxes. You can get in a decent pop at thirty miles an hour.

Three miles down the road lived my junior high school shop teacher. Mr Smith was a heavyset man, with grey hair and Coke-bottle eyeglasses. He wasn't a bad teacher, but he had an irresistible mailbox. Each time I smashed up his mailbox, he put in a new one. Finally, he installed one made of rubber. The baseball bat didn't do any good, so I—using a recipe from *The Anarchist Cookbook*—cooked up homemade napalm on my friend's kitchen stove, carried it in an old paint can and poured it all over the mailbox, which melted. Once more, my shop teacher couldn't get his letters delivered.

■

Some of the men in my life—my grandfather and J. W. in particular—had a lot of prejudices about blacks and Asians. One time, I was working in a donut store run by one of my aunts and my grandfather happened to be there when a number of black college students walked through the door. I was mortified to hear him mumble aloud about how he wished the Ku Klux Klan would come back. I noticed one of the students give him a withering look, as if to say, 'You are one pathetic loser.' I was relieved that he and his buddies got out the door without incident and, even though I loved my grandfather deeply, resolved not to be like him in that respect. I brought black friends by the house, and kept doing it even after he asked me to stop. 'Grandpa, you've got to get out of the 1950s,' I would tell him. 'It's the 1990s now.'

I think that fear of the unknown—blacks and Asians, in this case—led my grandfather to have those prejudices, and I would say that the very same fears made it easy for too many American soldiers—myself included—to abuse Iraqi civilians. In our training, our commanders taught us to demonise and hate Iraqis and Muslims. Looking back, I am sorry to admit that some of the negative parts of my own childhood climbed up from the darkness of my own soul and shook hands, in a way, with my army training. It took some time in Iraq before I could put the hateful thoughts behind me.

During my childhood, folks used to say that one day there would be another war between the north and the south. People sometimes wished that they could bring back the past, but I don't think they truly wanted war in their own back-yards. If they had any idea of what war meant—if they could picture blood spilling from white, black or any other bodies— I am quite sure they wouldn't have wanted it.

I learned this the hard way. In Iraq, the first time an inno-cent civilian died in front of me, I didn't ask myself questions about her racial or ethnic background. The only question to ask was why she had to die in the first place.

I think all the talk in Guthrie, about bringing back another war between the north and the south, was just a way to let out hot air, and no more than an ignorant way to shoot the breeze. I think that deep down, all people really wanted was to pass the time by watching—or joining—an old-fashioned fist fight. The summers were hot and God-awful boring, and there wasn't much to do in Guthrie except get drunk and start fighting. In that respect, I quickly became a model citizen.

I got in my first fight when I was eight, while at a football game. A thirteen-year-old boy started picking on a kid in my grade, so I kicked the bully in the face. He was a foot taller and a whole lot bigger. He blacked both of my eyes and busted my lip. I had another stepdad back then, and I feared that I would get a whupping for coming home beaten in a fight. When he came to pick me up, I pointed out the boy I had fought. My stepdad noticed his size and said I had done enough for the day.

I fought through junior high and kept fighting in high school. I fought black kids and I fought white. I even fought teammates on my football team. I fought so many times that my jaw still locks up from having taken so many punches.

When I was about seventeen, I got arrested for taking a swing at a police officer who tried to stop me from going to help my mother during a forest fire. My grandmother nearly got herself charged for barging into the police station, swearing at all the officers and demanding my release.

In court, the judge suspended the charges when he heard that the police officer had ganged up with other cops and roughed me up. My only requirement was to attend a few classes on anger management, which I did with two men who had gotten into all sorts of trouble. One of them had beaten up his ex-wife's boyfriend. Not long after the classes ended, I discovered the two of them yet again pounding the snot out of the ex-wife's boyfriend. At the time, I thought that anger management was a bit of a joke. Looking back, however, I think that everybody would have been better off if a few soldiers I know had been sent to anger management instead of Iraq.

These days, Brandi and I don't let our children play with toy guns. I see the irony in that. Zack, our eldest, is nine years old. When I was his age, one of my favourite pastimes was to stand alone in the backyard, blasting beer bottles apart with a .22 rifle. Because he came from another country, had an American accent and took some time fitting into a new Canadian school, Zack became the target of a bully. One of my biggest challenges as a father was *not* to tell him to cock his arm and slug the bully in the mouth. But I know that Zack will do better things in life and that the world will be a better place if he learns to use words to solve his problems.

My first experience of terrorism was in my own home state, and I know that 168 lives would have been saved if a man named Timothy McVeigh had been taught to use words instead of force.

In 1995, when the ex-soldier and war veteran blew up the

federal building in Oklahoma City, we felt the blast in our high school some twenty miles away. McVeigh used a truckload of ammonium nitrate—cowshit fertiliser, basically—to kill all those people, including nineteen children. A boy in my school lost his dad in the explosion, and a girl lost both of her parents. Before it happened, some of the kids had teased this girl about coming from a poor family. The teasing stopped after the explosion. I had no idea what to say to a person who had lost both her parents, so I just felt sorry for her and said nothing at all. Classes were cancelled as soon as we got the news. We assembled in school for the rest of the day to watch the television. Within forty-eight hours, police charged Timothy McVeigh with blowing up the building. I couldn't believe it. I had figured it was the work of a foreign terrorist. But it was an American, a former gunnery sergeant in the 1st Infantry Division in the Persian Gulf War, who had blown up his own people.

When I started going out with Brandi, she knew that I had gotten into my share of fights down by the Cimarron River, but her background was just as rough as mine. She had plenty of fights under her own belt, and had also been warned that she'd face consequences at home if she lost a fight in the streets.

I told her I had seen my mother get beaten too much, and that I would never beat a woman. She liked that about me. She liked everything about me. She was so like me that there was barely anything that needed explanation. We were both poor, had both grown up with way too much violence in our family, and both wanted to put the worst of our lives behind us. I knew, within five seconds of meeting her, that she wanted to be a good person and to lead a good life. I believe she felt the same way about me.

Brandi and I were both eighteen when we met. I was still in grade 12, but she had already graduated from high school and was working in a dollar store. The day after we met, I stopped by the store to ask her out to dinner. She accepted but persuaded me to forget the restaurant and settle on fast food. Why waste money, when we could park the pickup by a quiet creek, talk, look out at the water and let the night grow late?

Brandi liked my mother, but she could read J. W. like a book. She knew the score. When Brandi was three, her mother was murdered. At the time, her father had been serving a seven-year jail term.

J. W. tried to tell Brandi and me what we could and couldn't do in bed, but we didn't listen to him. It wasn't his trailer anyway, it was my mother's. To hell with his instructions that Brandi sleep on one side of a bedsheet, and that I sleep on the other.

Although I tried to have as little as possible to do with J. W., I liked his own father a little better. His name was Bill Church, and he had fought in the Korean War. He had been sprayed with tear gas in Korea and lost an eye. I tried to ask him about Korea, but he never wanted to talk about it. The last time I spoke to him was just before leaving for Iraq. He cried to hear the news that I was going to war. He said he understood that I had to go, but warned me to be careful.

I have seventeen cousins and various aunts and uncles and Brandi has relatives too, but we have hardly spoken to any of them since I deserted the army. With the exception of my mother and my brother, most of them are scandalised by what we have done. I believe they fear they'll have trouble with the law if they talk to us, and have written us out of the family.

Brandi and I lost more than just our country when we came with our children across the border at Niagara Falls, New York. We lost our families too.

Brandi and I agree that it was love at first sight. We were inseparable from the day that we met. Within two weeks, we made plans to get married. We wanted to save up and have a decent wedding, but we couldn't save enough to pay for it.

Brandi and I took an apartment together after I graduated from high school. We worked at every imaginable kind of job. Wherever we went, Brandi worked as a waitress and I held down jobs as a welder, general labourer, roofer, cook, salesperson and pizza delivery man. I usually made about $7 or $8 an hour. We moved all the time in search of better jobs and better pay. When things got too hard in Guthrie, we tried our luck in Oklahoma City. And then we tried Madison, Wisconsin. And then we moved back to Oklahoma City.

Zack, the first of our children, arrived in 1998 when we

were both twenty. In February 1999, Brandi and I gave up on our dreams for a family wedding and eloped to Arkansas. We were married by a justice of the peace. We had a crowd of four: Zack, Brandi's sister, her father and her stepmother. Brandi's folks took care of Zack during our one-night honeymoon. We stayed in a hotel in Muskogee, Oklahoma, and ordered in pizza.

By the time Adam came along in October of 1999, Brandi and I were finding it hard to live on her tips and on my salary. Changing cities and jobs never led to better pay. I picked up some welding work on some of the jobs, but got no formal training. To cut down on costs, we bought clothes at second-hand stores and stayed in rundown apartments. Our place in Oklahoma City had holes in the floor and in the windows. The water didn't run and the toilet didn't work. The place didn't even have a stove. Brandi had to go to her grandmother's home to cook for us.

Brandi had Oklahoma State health insurance for herself and our children, but I had none. One day I felt stabbing pains in the back and started urinating blood. I drove to a hospital in Oklahoma City, but they turned me down because I had no insurance. The next hospital I tried let me in and X-rayed a kidney stone but couldn't get it out. In that first of four hospital visits for kidney stone problems, I was billed for more than $2000. I couldn't pay it. Our debts started piling up while our credit rating sank. I still have the stone in me and it still acts up.

By the year 2000, when we were both twenty-two, Brandi

and I had become desperate. With two young boys, we didn't even have money to see the dentist. Our families were too poor to help much, but Brandi's grandmother sometimes gave us food. We never had as much as $50 in the bank. When we were living in Wisconsin, Brandi and I started talking about the military as a way to get out of poverty. I tried to enlist in the marines. But they turned me down because I had two children already and too many debts.

Brandi and I managed to keep going. By 2002, we were back in Oklahoma City. Brandi was looking after Zack and Adam, and Philip—our third child—was on the way. I had a job delivering pizza and was allowed to take home as much as I wanted for dinner. We got sick of pizza awfully fast.

I decided to try my luck once more with the military. This time, I would try the army. Maybe their standards wouldn't be as high. In March, I drove to the US Army recruiting station in Moore, Oklahoma. This time, at last, I found some good luck. Or so I thought.

# TWO

# RECRUITMENT AND TRAINING

I had driven past it many times before. The US armed services recruiting station was located in a strip mall in Moore, a suburb of Oklahoma City, not far from where the interstate highway I-240 meets Penn Street.

I didn't dress up to make an impression, that first day in the recruiting station. I felt better in my T-shirt and jeans. I had $10 in my pocket—just enough for milk and cigarettes—and Brandi had $40 at home, and that just about summed up our life savings that day. So even if I had wanted to dress up, there was no money for it.

Outside the recruiting station, someone had plastered posters promoting life in the armed forces. Every word of those posters seemed designed for people like me. I had no money, I had dreams of getting formal training as a welder, I needed to get my teeth fixed, and I wanted to have my kidney stones removed. If I only joined the military, the posters suggested, I would be on easy street. The armed forces were offering money for college tuition, health insurance, and even a cash bonus for signing up. To top it all off, military service would give me a chance to travel and discover a new way of life.

Brandi and I didn't like being in Oklahoma any more, and we wanted to get out. For folks like us who were poor and getting poorer by the day, the posters made me think that getting a job with the armed forces would be like winning the lottery. The difference, of course, was that almost nobody wins the lottery. But just about anybody can get into the armed forces—unless he or she is as poor as me.

It had been humiliating, two years earlier, to have been booted out of the marine recruiting centre, because of my debts and growing family. This time I would have to be honest about my situation, but I sure hoped they would take me.

When I walked in, I saw recruiters behind six desks. I walked up to a staff sergeant whose name was something along the lines of Van Houten.

He was a tall white man, heavyset, and looked like he was in his late twenties or early thirties.

'I'm thinking of joining the army,' I said.

Van Houten stood up and shook my hand.

'What's your name?'

'Joshua Key.'

'Can I call you Josh?'

I grinned. 'Everybody does.'

'Good Oklahoma boy, are you? Me too. Grew up not far from here.' He did have an Oklahoma accent. He pointed to a chair. 'Sit down, son, and make yourself comfortable. Hungry? Thirsty? We've got lots of stuff around here.'

'No thank you, I'm fine.'

'Well how about just coffee, then?'

'All right, coffee would be good.'

'What do you take in it?'

'One milk and five sugars.'

'You like a drop of caffeine with your sugar, do you?'

I grinned again. He called for someone to get me a coffee, just the way I had asked for it, and within a minute I held the steaming cup.

Van Houten had a stack of papers on his desk, and a pen in his hand.

'All right with you if I ask a few questions?' he said.

'Sure,' I said.

'That's good,' he said. 'Cause I have a lot of them.'

'Fine with me,' I said.

Van Houten began with the basics. What was my full name? Where did I live? Where and when was I born? What were the names of my father and mother, and where and when were they born? What was my education? Was I married? How many kids did I have?

I told him everything, but Van Houten slowed down a bit when we got to my family situation.

'What's your wife's name?'

'Brandi Key.'

'Maiden name?'

'Johnson.'

'And your kids?'

I told him about Zack and Adam, and said that we had a third child on the way.

He raised his finger, stopped me right there and spoke in a low, confidential tone.

'All right, not another word about your wife being pregnant. Is that understood? We leave that part out. You can't enlist if you've got three children, but if everything else checks out I can get you in, if we leave that part out.'

'Okay,' I said.

'And whatever you do,' he said, 'don't mention it to the commanding officer here.'

Van Houten offered to swing by my home to speak to Brandi about all the family benefits associated with life in the military, but he warned me to keep Brandi away from the recruiting station so that no superior military officers would notice her pregnancy. I got the message loud and clear.

Van Houten told me to keep one or two other details to myself as well. He would not take down information about the two herniated disks from a back injury because, he said, that could complicate my entry into military life. He didn't want me to say anything about my arrest at eighteen for assaulting a police officer.

When I began to raise the matter of my debts, he stopped me once more. 'I won't ask, and don't you tell,' he said.

Van Houten gave me the impression that, as a favour to me, he was leaving out all the details that might hurt my chances of getting into the military. He became my coach, my guidance counsellor, my adviser, my personal biographer, as well as the provider of coffee, donuts and submarine sandwiches over the next five or six weeks.

I had imagined that it would be possible to apply, be tested and checked out and sign up within a day or two, but the process stretched out for the better part of six weeks.

After completing the initial questionnaire, Van Houten told me to return at 5.30 am a few days later to take an aptitude test.

'Have a good meal, get a good sleep tonight, and eat breakfast before you come in for the test,' he said. 'You'll do better that way.'

I showed up on time and spent two hours on a question-and-answer test dealing with math, English, mechanical understanding and general knowledge.

There were about thirty young men and women in the room, and we all got our scores as soon as we finished the test. I was told that 30 was the passing score, and that 99 was the highest score possible. I got a 49, and saw to my amazement that not a single other person in the room had passed the test.

Van Houten told me that 49 was a good score, but that if I wanted I could take the test one more time to see if I could get a 50, which would give me more choices about where to go in the military. I took the test again, but got the same score.

One of Van Houten's colleagues, a short, thin, middle-aged government employee in civilian clothes named Daniel Russell, told me that I had three options. I could become an infantryman, a multiple launch rocket systems driver, or a bridge builder.

'Can I join work in the army without having to go overseas?' I said. 'I don't want to leave Brandi and the kids.'

'Absolutely,' Russell said. 'I can give you the bridge-building position in the continental United States. That means right here on the continent. You wouldn't even have to go to Hawaii or Alaska.

'Bridge builder sounds good to me,' I said.

Russell leaned forward and looked into my eyes. 'I can get you a $7000 signing bonus if you pick one of the other two.'

I asked him about the other positions. Working as an infantryman or as a multiple launch rocket systems driver meant combat duty, and I made it clear to Russell that I did not want to go into combat or leave my country.

'Think about it,' he said. 'Seven thousand dollars.'

'I don't have to think any more on that one, sir. I don't want to do combat duty. Not even for $7000. Tell me more about bridge building.'

Russell told me that the army employed many men to fix bridges in the continental United States. I would not receive any signing bonus, but I would be allowed to choose to go to a 'non-deployable' military base. 'Non-deployable', Russell explained, meant that it was a base that did not send men to war.

When I pressed for more information, Russell said that if I wanted to do bridge building, the closest military base was at Fort Carson, Colorado. I told him I had never heard of it. Russell explained that Fort Carson was in Colorado Springs, and home to a military unit called the 43rd Combat Engineer Company.

'But that sounds like combat,' I said.

'It sounds like that, but it isn't what you think,' Russell said. 'It's a non-deployable base, and you will be put to work building bridges in the United States. It's called Combat Engineer because you have to blow up bridges, sometimes, before you can build new ones.'

'So this means I can stay with my family, and don't have to go overseas?' I asked again.

'Soldier, it will be as easy as cheesecake. You're going to be building bridges from nine to five every day and spending every evening at home with your family.'

It sounded too good to be true. But to help put my mind at ease, Russell promised to write 'CONUS', short for 'Continental United States', right on my contract.

Our conversation ended there, and I felt a little more relaxed about my future in the army.

■

A week or two after I first showed up at the recruiting centre, Van Houten came to my home and won Brandi over immediately. Life on the military base was secure, he said. We wouldn't have to worry about violent criminals breaking into our home and hurting our children. We would stay in clean, decent accommodation that any working American would be proud of, he said. The rent would be free on base. (I learned later that this was not true, and that about $700 would be docked every month from my paycheck for the rent.)

The whole family would have access to comprehensive health insurance, he said, and I would be able to get up to $20,000 in tuition for college studies. I told Van Houten that I wanted training as a welder, and he said the money could be used for that, and that I could even begin college studies while posted to my military base.

Over the next several weeks, I had to see Van Houten nearly every day to take additional tests and to fill in more paperwork. Every time I arrived at the recruiting station he offered me something to eat. What's more, he offered to take me along when he went jogging and weight training in the gym of the nearby Tinker Air Force Base. I accepted, and joined him some thirty times at the gym. On each trip, he bought me coffee and sandwiches.

Van Houten offered up a little information about himself, too. He was married and had three children and came from Lawton, Oklahoma. He was looking forward to returning to his regular military job as a surveyor at Fort Sill, Oklahoma, but for the time being he was stuck recruiting young

Americans and working on a quota system. I can't remember exactly how many men he said he was required to recruit, but I believe it was about one person per week.

He was stressed-out about it, and said he couldn't wait to return to his former job as a military surveyor. 'They rip up my ass if I don't make my quota,' he said.

For my medical and physical tests, I peed in a cup, gave blood and was made to walk like a duck—knees bent and squatting low with my butt near the ground. I asked about that, and was told that the test would indicate if I was flat-footed. Apparently, you cannot get into the military with flat feet. It seemed that they gave me every vaccination known to mankind, including eight shots against anthrax.

Because I spent a lot of time in the recruiting and related military buildings, I had the chance to notice all sorts of details. By my estimation, about half of the applicants were black, one-quarter Latino, and one-quarter white. I was almost twenty-four when I applied, and I felt old compared with most of the applicants who appeared to be teenagers. Young men and women who were just seventeen were allowed to join if they had permission from their parents. I would say that about three-quarters of the applicants were men, and one-quarter women.

One day a teenage girl walked in and began to apply for entry to the army. A little later, a lieutenant colonel in military apparel burst through the door. All the soldiers and non-commissioned officers in the room jumped to their feet to salute him. Somebody whispered to me that he was in the marines. He swept by us all, grabbed his daughter by the arm, shouting for all of us to hear: 'There is no goddamn way that any daughter of mine is joining the fucking army.' He dragged her out the door, and that was the last I saw of her. I had heard that marines and soldiers hated each other, but this was the first time I saw the emotion expressed openly.

Another time, at a military entrance processing station—a separate building to which I often had to go as my application inched forward—I saw a poster on a wall that read: 'Desertion in the time of war means death by a firing squad.'

A young man and woman were standing under the poster and I watched them carefully.

'Oh my God,' she said, 'can they really do that?'

I wondered the same thing, as I was made to sign a paper saying that I had read and understood the poster.

Finally, in mid-April 2002—just a month shy of my twenty-fourth birthday—I learned from Van Houten that the army had cleared all of my medical tests and paperwork. I was fit to join the United States army, he said, and I would do my country proud. He explained that I would receive $1200 a month in salary and commit to a three-year contract. He did not tell me what I would only learn later—that the army could recall me any time it wanted to up to seven years after I signed up.

One last time, before signing, I asked Van Houten for reassurances that I would not be sent into combat and that I would be allowed to live with my family and work for the army in the United States.

'If World War III breaks out and they are sending everybody overseas, then you could be required to do duty as well,' he said. 'But even then, it would be unlikely. Because of your growing family, you would be the last person to be sent overseas.'

That seemed reasonable to me.

To seal the deal, Staff Sergeant Van Houten looked me eye to eye, man to man, shook my hand and said, 'Soldier, you ain't got anything to worry about. You're going to be building bridges in the continental United States and be home with your family every evening.'

Two other non-commissioned officers looked over my shoulder, turned the pages of the contract, skipped over the fine print and pointed out all the Xs where I was to sign my name. I signed where they pointed, and believed what I was told.

I was a bloody fool to do so.

On 13 April 2002 I entered into a contract with the United States army. Eighteen days later, I was sent to basic training in Fort Leonardwood, Missouri.

I took a commercial flight from Oklahoma City to St Louis. At the airport, I met up with about 150 other new recruits. We boarded a number of military buses. It was a long drive to Fort Leonardwood, but at least I was on the military payroll now. Brandi—who went to live with our boys in Chetoca, Oklahoma—would be able to buy the children some clothes, and we would all eat a little better.

We pulled into Fort Leonard around 3 am. As we prepared to disembark, a long line of drill sergeants waited in line. They shouted that that we had to get off the bus immediately, screamed that we were worthless assholes, and hollered that anything could be changed in the contracts we had signed and any promises made to us could now be thrown out the window.

The drill sergeants held megaphones as we all scrambled to get out. 'Get the fuck out!' they screamed right in our faces.

Like the others, I was nervous and scared, but I knew— even amidst all the pushing and the shouting—that they were just trying to break us down mentally, and that more of this would come.

We had to give up our cigarettes, lighters, scissors and nail files. We were taken to the barracks, allowed to sleep for an hour, rushed to a mess hall and given one minute to eat. And I mean one minute.

I wolfed down the scrambled eggs as fast as I could.

A day after our arrival, I was allowed to call Brandi. I only had a minute or two on the telephone with her, and I wouldn't be given another chance to call her for seventeen weeks. Quickly, I let her know that they did not let us have coffee or tea in boot camp and that she should send me some over-the-counter uppers called Yellow Jackets. You can't get them any longer but back then they were perfectly legal, and you could buy them at any gas station or drugstore in Oklahoma.

Ever the dutiful wife, Brandi slipped the Yellow Jackets inside a box of Zest soap, put the bar of soap back inside and sent it to me by mail. Every morning, I swallowed a pill to jolt myself awake.

Within a day or two of arriving at Fort Leonardwood, while I stood at attention with 300 other recruits, a drill sergeant hollered out that we had been put into the 35th Combat Engineer Company and that we would learn to be 'the most devious goddamn killers on the battlefield'.

I didn't know exactly what that meant, but it sure didn't sound like bridge building. I tried not to worry about it, because I still believed that after boot camp I would be sent to a non-deployable military base. So, to my way of thinking, it did not matter if I learned about grenades and mines because I wouldn't have to use them in combat anyway.

I turned twenty-four just a few days after arriving at boot camp. I didn't tell anybody, because I didn't want to draw any attention to myself. If anybody notices you or stops to speak to you at boot camp, it's bad news for sure. The name of the game is to stay out of sight of anybody in any position to rain down any punishment. When sergeants blew horns and banged trash cans at two in the morning, hauled us out of bed and made us each do 100 pushups, I tried to struggle through it and to stay under the radar screen.

I shared a bunk bed with a private named Babbit, who was steaming over a lie he had swallowed during recruitment.

The poor sucker had been a story like mine—but even more ridiculous. A recruiter in Lawrence, Kansas, had promised Babbit that if he signed up for service, the army would reward him and his girlfriend with a holiday to Korea. When Babbit got to Fort Leonardwood and found out that his Korean junket had disappeared about as fast as my bridge-building promise, his girlfriend dumped him.

'When I get back home I'm going to find that recruiter and tell him that he's a lying piece of shit,' Babbit fumed.

Among the 300 recruits, I would say that a third of us where white, another third black and another third Latino. There were just two women. As we went through the seventeen weeks of basic training, we were shouted at, insulted, awoken and kept off balance by sergeants whose job it was to break us down and build us back up in their own mould.

If somebody failed to do something properly, every recruit in the company would be punished. That quickly taught us to hate laggards and people who just couldn't follow orders fast enough.

I must say that I loved boot camp.

I was good with guns, didn't mind the exercise, and felt myself swell with patriotism and pride when our commanders told us that Americans were the only decent people on the planet, and that Muslims and terrorists all deserved to die.

One day, all 300 of us lined up in the bayonet range, each facing a life-sized dummy that we were told to imagine was a Muslim man.

As we stabbed the dummies with our bayonets, one of our commanders stood on a podium and shouted into a microphone: 'Kill! Kill! Kill the sand niggers.'

We, too, were made to shout out 'Kill the sand niggers!' as we stabbed the heads, then the hearts, and then slashed the throats of our imaginary victims.

While we shouted and stabbed, drill sergeants walked among us to make sure that we were all shouting. It seemed that the full effect of the lesson would be lost on us, unless we shouted out the words of hate as we mutilated our imaginary enemies.

I shouted as loud and stabbed as mercilessly as any man on the range, and I slowly began to feel that I was somebody important. I was no longer a fast-food delivery man earning a pittance for a wage plus tips and all of the pizza I could eat. I was no longer wondering how I could possibly put enough food on the table for Brandi and the boys. I was now an American soldier, and proud to think of myself as a perfect killing machine. I felt patriotic and invincible. I believed every word I was told, including that it was the job of the American army to keep order in the world.

Our commanders told us that people who were not Americans were 'terrorists' and 'slant eyes'. They said that Muslims were responsible for the September 11 attacks on our country, that the people of Afghanistan were 'terrorist pieces of shit that all deserved to die'.

Commanders also drilled these beliefs into us by making us memorise and call out various chants.

I have trouble remembering their precise words, though one of them went something like this:

> One shot
> One kill
> One Arab
> One Asian

Another had to do with putting our skills as sappers, or makers and defusers of bombs, to good use:

> Who can take a shopping mall
> And fill it full of people?
> The sapper daddy can,
> Cause he takes a lot of pains
> And makes the hurt go good.

> Who can take all the people in the mall
> And chop 'em up with Uzis?
> The sapper daddy can,
> Cause he takes a lot of pains
> And makes the hurt go good.

Iraqis, in the mouths of the officers and soldiers of the United States Army, were never Iraqis. And Muslims were never civilians. Nobody once mentioned the word 'civilian' in the same breath as Iraq, when I trained to become a soldier. Iraqis, I was taught to believe, were not civilians and they were not even people. We had our own terms for them. Our commanders called them rag heads, so we did the same. We called them Habibs. We called them sand niggers. We called them hajjis, and it wasn't until I was sent to war that a man in

Iraq explained to me that 'hajji' was a complimentary term for a Muslim who had made the pilgrimage to Mecca. In training, all I knew was a 'hajji' was someone to be despised. The hajjis, Habibs, rag heads and sand niggers were the enemy, and they were not to be thought of with a shred of humanity. No wonder my wife and I both thought, by the time I flew overseas to war, that all Muslims were terrorists and all terrorists were Muslims and that the only solution was to kill as many Iraqis as possible.

There is one other thing I was taught in at Fort Leonardwood that chipped away at my soul and that made it that much easier, a year or so later, for me to accept and take part in the violence that my fellow soldiers dished out to civilians in Iraq.

Twice during my time at boot camp, one of my drill sergeants by the name of Johnson made me get up from my bed in the middle of the night, collect one or two aides, and beat up recruits who were falling behind in their duties or failing to comply with orders.

Sergeants, I was told, were not allowed to beat up trainees. So they used me to do their dirty work, and I, stupidly, felt honoured to do exactly as they said.

The first time, Sergeant Johnson sent me to beat up a trainee named Taylor, who had lunged at a drill sergeant and tried to start a fight with him. My buddies and I threw a blanket over his head and beat his chest and ribs with a sock stuffed with soap. I whacked him hard while he cried out in pain. 'You been making trouble for all of us and there will be more of this tomorrow if you keep it up,' I said.

After taking my licks, Taylor didn't try to start any more fights with non-commissioned officers.

But a little while later, Sergeant Johnson sent me out again to beat up a recruit by the name of Armstrong who had been refusing to take orders. Once more, my buddies and I jumped on him in the night, covered his head and pummelled his body. Armstrong screamed during the whole beating, and kept screaming when we left. I had to run back and threaten to beat him again if he didn't shut up. He fell silent after that, but in the morning, I saw that my intimidation tactics had not worked.

When we were woken in the morning, Armstrong began shouting to anyone who would listen that he would not get out of bed and that he would not follow orders. The drill sergeants took him away and I never saw him again. I heard that he was let out of the army, although I don't know if it was true. At the time, I thought of him as a weakling and a coward who was an embarrassment to the army.

I enjoyed boot camp. I liked the challenge involved in setting and defusing landmines. It was fun to learn how to set off bombs using plastic explosives and TNT. One day, well into our training, we were rewarded for our hard work with the opportunity to set off a bomb consisting of about two hundred pounds of C-4 explosives. After hiding inside a bunker a distance of a few hundred yards, we ignited the bomb.

The blast roared in our ears, and the earth shook. I felt the vibrations rolling through my body. Dirt and debris flew through the air, and I found it all exciting. I had never witnessed such a powerful explosion in my life, found the experience exhilarating, and hoped I would get to make another bomb and see it explode.

I loved shooting on the practice range, and earned a pin for my good marksmanship. When we were tested in rigging and defusing bombs, I got top grades in my company. After nine weeks of basic training, five weeks of sapper training and three more weeks of training in how to drive tanks and armoured personnel carriers, I moved to my permanent military station at Fort Carson.

In October of 2002, Brandi, the boys and I moved into a modest row-house on the new base. I still believed that Fort Carson was a 'non-deployable' base that did not send soldiers to war—but that last bubble burst within minutes of my arrival.

A specialist named Abby was sent to pick me up at the reception area on base. When he showed up, he said that I would be joining the 43rd Combat Engineer Company.

'Since the 1800s, we've been in every major war the United States has fought and we're proud of it,' he said.

I was shocked, but said nothing as he drove me to my barracks.

Over the next days, I learned that I had been placed in the third squad of the first platoon of the 43rd CEC, as it was called. Each squad had about six or seven members, so there were about twenty people in a platoon. There were six platoons in the 43rd CEC, and about 120 men in total. Most of us were combat engineers, trained in how to make and defuse bombs and mines. Our company was part of the Second Squadron of the 3rd Armored Cavalry Regiment. The 3rd ACR had its own distinguished wartime history. Known also as the 'Brave Rifles', soldiers with the 3rd ACR had fought in the American Civil War, the Spanish–American War, both world wars and the Persian Gulf War, among others. One of the 3rd ACR's most famous and colourful generals was George S. Patton Jr., who, during World War II favoured ivory-handled colt .45 revolvers and travelled with a bull terrier named Willie.

Shortly after arriving at Fort Carson, I paid a visit one afternoon to the office of Lieutenant Joyce and found him sitting in his chair.

'Do I have permission to speak, Sir?'

'Yes, Soldier.'

'Sir, when I joined the military I was told I was being sent to a non-deployable base. But I hear that the 43rd Combat Engineer Company is a combat company. Is there some way we can fix this problem, so I can be sent to a non-deployable unit?'

'Soldier, you obviously don't understand the military way of life. Get the hell out of my office.'

I felt that everything was lost, and that I should get out of his office before I made matters worse for myself. I paid for that complaint.

The next morning, my squad leader Staff Sergeant Padilla shouted in my face.

'You broke rank by speaking to Lieutenant Joyce and you're a fucking piece of shit.'

The team leader at the time, Specialist Abby, continued with the endless stream of insults. I was 'smoked', as they say, for several days. They made me do pushups, duck walks, crawl around on my hands and knees and stand at attention while every man in my platoon hollered that I was 'a useless asshole' and a 'stupid shit'.

We have an expression in the army: 'drink water, drive on'. It means that when things get bad, you just have to suck it up and keep going. When I learned that I was in a combat-ready army company and that I was surely to be sent to war at some point, I felt that I had no choice but to take it and keep going.

I felt humiliated to be taking abuse from every man in my platoon. I wanted to fit in and be respected. I wanted, one day, to be promoted to the rank of sergeant. I wanted them to see how fast and steady I was with my hands. Whether it came to shooting rifles, planting bombs, defusing mines or driving trucks, I knew that I had fantastic hands and sensed that they only way to earn their respect was to show them how good I really was. I could put a mine in the ground and take it back out within a minute or so.

Sure enough, the abuse and insults continued until we were out on a demonstration range a week or two after my arrival in Fort Carson. The fall weather had turned cold, and we were using a heater to stay warm in the field. But the heater stopped working, and all the men started getting cold. After I fixed the alternator and restored heat for my platoon buddies, I earned the name 'MacGyver'—after the inventive television character—and was never called a shit bag again. I 'drank water and drove on'.

I could never quite follow my instructions to rank the army first, God second and family third in my own personal priorities, but I did my best to fit in and prove myself in the six months that passed before we were told to say goodbye to our families and to pack our bags for war.

# THREE
# EARLY DAYS IN IRAQ

I believed the reasons that President George W. Bush gave for beginning the second Iraq War on 20 March 2003. I had faith in my country and accepted what I was told: Iraq was stockpiling weapons of mass destruction and harbouring the terrorists behind the 9/11 attacks on the United States.

I accepted the argument that it was time to overthrow Saddam Hussein and bring democracy to Iraq. I wasn't eager to fight, but I would follow my commanders. After all, I thought, it was better for me to help stomp out terrorism and defend America than to leave the job to my own children.

When Operation Iraqi Freedom began, I was a private first class in the American army, stationed in Fort Carson, Colorado with the 43rd Combat Engineer Company. We were a company of 120 men trained in landmines and explosives. Although our tanks and other military equipment had been shipped to the Middle East long before the offensive began, I suspected that we might not be sent into action. Soldiers in my platoon talked all the time about how, in the first Persian Gulf War in 1991, it had only taken the American ground offensive 100 hours to drive the Iraqis out of Kuwait.

Staff Sergeant Padilla, one of the non-commissioned officers in my squad, said not to worry about going to war. He said he had gone to the first Persian Gulf War, but had simply waited for months in the Arabian desert, far from combat at all times. It would probably be more of the same this time, he told me.

I gave my wife similar reassurances. 'It will be over before they can lift our butts into the air,' I told Brandi.

But Sergeant Padilla and I were both wrong. On 10 April, just three weeks after the American offensive began, I left for war with my company. We flew from Colorado Springs to Frankfurt, and then to Kuwait. I barely slept on the flights, and kept wondering what I would be doing in Iraq. I expected that I'd be using my military training in explosives, clearing the Iraqi desert of landmines so that American tanks could roll safely by. Leaving the plane in Kuwait, we boarded buses on the tarmac. On route to the military camp, I couldn't keep

my eyes from drifting to the television screen on the bus.
'Teletubbies' was playing—in Arabic. This was the first of
many surprises during my time in the Middle East.

We stayed about two weeks at Camp Illinois in the Kuwaiti
desert. We were rationed to one MRE (Meal, Ready to Eat)
and one litre of water per day, but Sergeant Lindsay—who
was in charge of my platoon—ordered us to steal water left at
night outside tents belonging to other army companies. I
wondered about the surprise and anger that would break out
among the soldiers who woke up to discover that they had no
water in the desert. But as a private first class I was on the
bottom of the chain of command, and anxious to prove
myself. I took the water without getting caught. Shortly
thereafter, Sergeant Lindsay gave me a similar order. At
night, when others were sleeping, I was to steal lights from
other companies. Once more, I managed to do it without
getting caught. After stealing them, I hooked up the lights
to generators so that we could see inside our own tents at
night.

During our time in the camp, I was sent to Kuwait City to
help unload Abrams tanks from ships and get them lined up
on flatbed trucks to be taken across the desert.

I was excited to see a bit of the city—especially all the
people driving Ferraris and Lamborghinis—and I got carried
away while driving the tanks. In a stupid moment, I tried
spinning a tank around in a circle, just to feel how well it
manoeuvred. In doing so, I crashed into another tank. An air
force officer saw the crash, but she then looked the other way.

Luckily for me, the last thing she wanted was to be dragged into writing accident reports. I got away from there as fast as I could, walking with one hand on my chest—directly over my name and rank—so that I couldn't be identified and disciplined later.

On 27 April, we packed up our things at Camp Illinois and began a long, fourteen-hour journey across the desert to Iraq. Our long convoy consisted of hundreds of flatbed trucks carrying about a thousand men from various military companies, as well as humvees, Abrams tanks and armoured personnel carriers (APCs). We moved at a snail's pace—about 20 miles per hour. I sat up with one of the truck drivers, and along the way looked out at blown-up tanks and discarded vehicles with bones strewn about them.

Somewhere inside Iraq, our convoy divided into smaller pieces. Our company of 120 men was sent alone into Ramadi. It would be our job to relieve the 82nd Airborne Division and to take control of the city of some 300,000 people. I was terrified, and expected that we would be driving straight into a war zone. I imagined Iraqi soldiers launching grenades and spraying bullets, and it didn't seem possible to me that such a small group of Americans could defend themselves in the city. However, on entering Ramadi, we were greeted with waves and cheers. Children racing up towards our vehicles shouted for food and water. So far, at least, this was the last thing from a war zone.

I was a member of the third squad of the first platoon of my company, and I travelled with my six squad mates in our

APC. It was about the length of a four-door car, and the width of a lane of traffic. Made of steel, but it lacked the thickness of a tank, or the durability to resist rocket-propelled grenades. There was room for four or so men below, and for another two or three up top to operate machine guns.

From the moment I entered Iraq, I was obsessed by the thought of being caught inside a burning tank. I preferred to risk sniper fire and sit on top of the vehicle. In Iraq, whenever I travelled on our APC, I always took my position on top, monitoring the streets and the rooftops with my M-249 automatic weapon ready. The M-249 weighs thirty-six pounds fully loaded. It is formally called a squad automatic weapon, but we called it a SAW, for short, because—at 2000 rounds a minute—it would saw right through any person it hit. Like the others, I was warned to shoot if I felt threatened and to ask questions later.

I was scared out of my wits that first day in Ramadi. Our own air force had just finished bombing these people, but as soon as we got out of our vehicles, we began patrolling their streets, on foot. With nearly one hundred pounds of weaponry, equipment and clothing on my back, I was about as mobile as a cow. It was just my platoon, twenty guys, walking single-file through streets full of Iraqis. I could not stop thinking that anywhere, at any time, some half-starved sniper on a roof could have taken me out in no time flat. Iraqi kids surrounded me in swarms, hands out, asking for water and food.

I kept hearing the last words my wife, Brandi, said to me before I flew out of Colorado Springs: 'Don't you let those terrorists near you, Josh. Even if they are kids. Get 'em before they get you.'

I also kept thinking about my officers' repeated warnings: 'If you feel threatened, kill first and ask questions later.'

And then there were the army chants buzzing through my head—chants we'd picked up in Fort Carson while we learned the ins and outs of blowing things up with C-4 explosives.

> Take a playground,
> Fill it full of kids,
> Drop on some napalm,
> And barbecue some ribs.

On that first day in Ramadi, when I saw kids coming at us from every direction with noses running and hands out-stretched, I felt surrounded by Muslims, terrorists, bomb-throwers and killers. They came in all sizes, of that I was sure. Why not children too?

In Ramadi, my platoon set up camp just a stone's throw from the Euphrates River, in a bombed-out palace. There was marble everywhere: on the floors, walls and pillars. I saw a destroyed elevator and a tiled mural of Saddam Hussein. The former groundskeeper ran up to us and said the palace had once belonged to Saddam Hussein himself. He was an older man who didn't appear to have anything to do, or any work to keep him going. He stayed near our troops to run errands and fetch drinks for the sergeants, for what I presumed was a little pocket change.

I unrolled my sleeping bag on the floor, about one hundred feet from an unexploded US bomb that sat half-buried in the floor, sticking out about six feet. It didn't seem like a safe place to be, but at least I had a roof over my head.

I ate my ration—a beef enchilada—and tried to smother the flavour with Tabasco sauce. Most of the other soldiers had no interest in the one-ounce shots of hot sauce that came with their MREs, so I scooped them up and used double and triple doses every time I ate. Oklahoma isn't far from Mexico, and an Oklahoma boy needs his hot sauce. Sometimes, in the boredom and fatigue of life in Iraq, hoarding and gulping down Tabasco sauce became a diversion in itself.

I remember still being hungry when I went to sleep that first night in Ramadi. There were no bombs dropping or mortars falling but I was awakened at 3 am and told to get my ass up quickly, because in one hour we going to raid a house full of terrorists.

We had a few minutes of orientation on the grounds of the palace. Captain Conde and some sergeants showed me and my squad mates a satellite photo of a house, and a drawing of the layout inside. Our assignment was to blow off the door, burst into the house, raid it fast and raid it good—look for contraband, caches of weapons, signs of terrorists or terrorist activity, round up the men and get out of there damn fast. The longer we stayed in any one location, the longer somebody would have to put us in the sights of a rocket-propelled grenade, or lob mortars at us.

I had no idea what to expect. Would I charge through the door, only to be blown to bits by a grenade? Would somebody with an AK-47 knock my Oklahoman ass right back out that door? Would some six-year-old terrorist with two days of gun training be waiting to put me in his cross-hairs? The minutes ticked on, and I wanted the hour to speed forward so we could get to our destination and get on with it.

One or two of the guys did pushups to pump themselves up. I borrowed Specialist Mason's portable CD player and bombed out my eardrums to the beat of Ozzy Osborne. It got me going. High, and ready for action. I topped that up by knocking back one or two more bottles of Tabasco sauce, which gave me a nice jolt. In Iraq, Tabasco sauce became my own little wake-up call, my own little hit to get me going.

I checked my watch, wished it would accelerate, and stuck some dip—Copenhagen, bourbon flavour—behind my lip. You can't manage a cigarette when you've got an M-249 automatic weapon on your arm. So dip was best. Makes your mouth black as sin, and rots the roots right out of your gums, but dip was my nicotine hit of choice going into that raid.

I committed our pre-raid instructions to memory. I knew the angles of the house, what door I would help blow down, how many floors were in the house, and who would do what when we busted inside. I would be third in the door—which means I was the second most likely to get shot, if anybody had a mind to take us down—and would head to the left. Always, for every raid, I would be third in, heading left.

I gripped my M-249. Yes, it could belt out 2000 rounds a minute, but only in theory. You couldn't really hold your finger down that long. Blazing away like that, the bullets turned the barrel as hot as Hades. If you held your finger down too long, it would warp the barrel.

It was time to go. We went out into the cool Iraqi night. We took a civilian vehicle—a white Toyota truck—so that the Iraqis would not suspect we were coming. Sergeant Fadinetz was at the wheel. He had a map with exact directions, including information about where to park the truck. Also in the truck was our squad leader, Sergeant Padilla, as well as Sergeant Jones, Specialist Sykora, another grunt, and me. We had our basic moves plotted out, like a set play in football. We drove into an upscale Iraqi neighbourhood, passed a mosque, and stopped near an attractive three-storey house.

We parked and ran out. It took thirty seconds for Sergeant Jones and me to put the charge of C-4 plastic explosive on the door. Then we dashed around to the side of the house, so we wouldn't blow ourselves up. You wouldn't want to be standing anywhere near that door when we blew it in. You'd be fried meat, if you were near the explosion.

I set off the blast, and then the six of us charged into the house. Sergeant Jones went first—that skinny, red-haired Ohio boy was always hot to trot. Next went Sergeant Fadinetz. Then me. After me came Sergeant Padilla. And after him came Specialist Sykora, who gobbled up professional wrestling like it was going out of style—that, and porn videos; even in Iraq, the man got his hands on porn videos regularly. After Sykora came another grunt from our squad. It was either Specialist Mason or Private First Class Lewis—I can't remember which of them was with me on that first raid.

With Sergeant Jones leading the way, we burst into the house. We were armed to the hilt. Kevlar helmets, flak jackets, machine guns, combat boots, the whole nine yards.

I'd never been inside an Iraqi's house before. We charged through a kitchen. I had been told by Sergeant Padilla to check everything, so I even opened the fridge. Perhaps, I thought, I would find guns or grenades hidden inside. No such luck. All I saw in there was a bit of food. In the freezer, I found big slabs of meat, uncovered. No wrapping. No plastic. Frozen, just like that. We ran into a living room with long couches, one along each wall. In this room with the abundance of couches we found two children, a teenage girl and a woman. We also found two young men in the house. One looked in his teens and the other perhaps in his early twenties—brothers.

We hollered and cussed. I spat dip on the floor and screamed along with the other soldiers at the top of my lungs. I knew they didn't understand, but I hollered anyway.

'Get down,' I shouted. 'Get the fuck down! Shut the fuck up!'

They didn't know what 'get down' meant, so we knocked the two brothers to the floor, face down. We put our knees on their backs, pulled their hands behind, and faster than you can bat an eye, we zipcuffed them. Zipcuffs are plastic handcuffs that lock on tight. They must have bit something fierce into those young men's skin. There was no key, nothing—the only way to get them off was to slice them off with cutters.

We pushed the brothers outside, where twelve other

soldiers from our platoon were waiting. Some loaded the Iraqi men onto the back of a truck. Others were 'pulling perimeter', which meant keeping guard to make sure that nobody entered or left the house or the surrounding area.

The Iraqi brothers were taken away to an American detention facility for interrogation. I don't know what it was called, and I don't know where it was. All I know is that we sent away every man—pretty well every male over five feet tall—that we found in our house raids, and I never saw one of them return to the neighbourhoods we patrolled regularly.

Inside, we kept on ransacking the house. The more obvious it became that we would find no weapons or contraband, the more we kicked the stuffing out of the house.

We knocked over dressers, sliced into mattresses with knives, kicked our way through doors, raided the three bedrooms on the second floor and raced up to the third floor. Would we find terrorists or nasty weapons stashed there? Nope. It was basically just a landing that led to a rooftop area where the family had washed clothes and hung them to dry.

We turned over everything we could and broke furniture at random, searching for contraband, weapons, proof of terrorist activity and signs of weapons of mass destruction.

We found nothing but a CD. Soldiers initially said it showed proof of terrorist activity, but it turned out to have nothing on it but a bunch of speeches by Saddam Hussein.

I figured that the terrorists had managed to dance out of our way that night, but that we'd nab them the next time.

Once we had everybody outside the house and had done

our initial job of ransacking, another squad took over inside. They kept raising hell in there, breaking and turning over more furniture, looking for weapons that we might have missed.

Outside, under a carport (a parking space under a roof, but no walls or enclosure) I was assigned to watch the women and children. We weren't arresting them, but we weren't allowing them to go anywhere either. The family members couldn't go back inside, and they couldn't wander off into the neighbourhood. They had to stay right there while we tore the hell out of their house.

The teenage girl started staring at me. I tried to ignore her. Then she started speaking to me. Inside, when we had been screaming at her and the others, I had assumed that nobody understood a word of English. But this young girl spoke to me in English, and her eyes bored holes right through me. She was skin and bones, not even a hundred pounds, not yet a full-grown woman, but something about her seemed powerful and disturbing.

I feared that girl, and I wanted to get away from her as fast as I could, but it was my job to stay right there and make sure that she didn't move. I had my weapon ready. She was wearing a blue nightgown, and had a white scarf covering her hair. She had no veil, so I could see her face perfectly. Her eyes were coal-black and full of hatred.

In English, she asked me: 'Where are you taking my brothers?'

'I don't know, Miss,' I said.

'Why are you taking them away?'

'I'm afraid I can't say.'

'When are you bringing them back?'

'Couldn't tell you that either.'

'Why are you doing this to us?'

I couldn't answer that.

I hoped that she did not raise a fuss. I didn't want her to start screaming, which could attract the attention of my squad mates. One or two of them, I feared, would be more than happy to use a rifle butt to knock out her teeth.

I hadn't been in Iraq more than twenty-four hours, and already I was having strange feelings.

First, I was vulnerable, and didn't like it. Even with all these soldiers and all this equipment, I knew that anywhere, at any time, any enterprising Iraqi with a gun, a wall to hide behind, and one decent eye could pick me off faster than a hawk nabs a mouse. Second, with hardly one foot into the war in Iraq, I was also uneasy about what we were doing here. Something was amiss. We hadn't found anything in this girl's house, but we had taken away her brothers and had busted it up pretty well in thirty minutes. Inside, another squad was still ransacking the house.

I didn't enjoy being stuck guarding this girl under the carport, in the cool April air before dawn in Ramadi. Her questions haunted me, and I didn't like not being able to answer them—even to myself.

I dared not speak to her any more, because that would amount to 'fraternising with the enemy'—something about which I would be warned many times in Iraq.

In the days to come I tried to drive that girl out of my mind. We hadn't found a thing in her house except slabs of meat in the fridge and a Saddam Hussein CD. No matter. We'd catch the terrorists the next day, to be sure. Or so I told myself.

We were pumped after that raid. It felt like a pouch of adrenaline was slung on an IV, dripping straight into my veins. It was one of the most exciting things I had ever done. After the first hit, I wanted more. I wanted to catch those fucking terrorists, and figured it was only bad luck that prevented us from nabbing them the first time.

■

We were told that the purpose of the house raids was to nab terrorists and to find evidence of terrorism. During that first month in Ramadi, we usually raided at least one home—and sometimes as many as four—each night. The houses we raided were ordinary, one- or two-storey homes in residential areas. They were far more attractive, spacious and comfortable than the trailer, apartments and houses I had inhabited in Oklahoma. Most of the houses in Iraq looked neat, tidy and well arranged—before we showed up. Our raids always took place in the middle of the night, to catch people sleeping and to intimidate them.

My whole platoon, consisting of about twenty officers and soldiers, would take part in the house raids. Twelve or so soldiers would place themselves outside, six positioned as guards and another six stationed at the trucks used to take away all the men—or any boys over five feet—that we found inside.

It was always the job of my squad of six or seven men to begin the raid itself. I was usually the one to put the plastic explosives on the door, set the charge and blow down the door. I never saw a person killed in a house raid, but if any Iraqi had been standing just inside their front door at the moment that I blew it off, they would certainly have been killed.

When we burst in the door, sometimes we raced through the house and found people in bed. At other times men and women were standing or sitting inside, looking completely stunned. Sometimes their hands would fly to their mouths. Sometimes they would start screaming. We would scream at them to get down, and knock down the men as quickly as we could so they could be zipcuffed and taken out to our waiting trucks. Any male who took his time about getting to the floor, or who protested loudly, would be given a quick rifle butt to the head or the stomach. I dished out my fair share of licks in those first raids.

Although I lived in terror for the first month or two that somebody would ambush us in the midst of a house raid—throwing grenades, or lighting us up with machine-gun fire—nobody ever resisted with as much as a finger. Looking back, with twelve American soldiers stationed outside and six more charging into the house, each one armed to the hilt and ready to shoot, I can see that resistance would have been suicide for any Iraqi. Even though no one tried to shoot us or made any effort to hurt us, it was common for American soldiers to beat the civilians.

At least every two or three days during my time in Iraq, I saw our soldiers kicking Iraqi civilians in the ribs and punching their faces until blood ran from their noses, mouths or eyebrows. Beating the snot out of an Iraqi civilian. I'm not proud to say that I participated in these beatings, but I was far less extreme than some of the soldiers. As time went on I lost any appetite for the beatings and refrained from them entirely.

We got the men outside as fast as we could, and it usually took longer to round up the women and children. The women would sometimes scream at us, and we would shout right back at them to 'shut the fuck up'. Sometimes they spoke English and sometimes they didn't. Often, we had no idea what they were saying and the only language of ours that they understood was our pointed machine guns.

Inside the houses, we knocked over garment closets, kicked in doors, ripped through mattresses and threw bookshelves to the floor. We broke locks off furniture, ripped drawers from dressers, threw over refrigerators and broke lanterns and lamps. Radios and televisions were thrown around and smashed.

In the first raid, the second, the third and the fourth, I wondered why we never managed to find anything. We tore hell out of those places, but inspite of all our ransacking, we never found anything other than the ordinary goods that normal people keep in their houses.

We commonly found AK-47s in the course of our raids—just as commonly as one might expect to find guns in houses in Guthrie, Oklahoma—and we didn't consider this unusual or evidence of terrorism. Initially, we confiscated every weapon we found. But after several weeks, Sergeant Padilla told us to stop taking them because Iraqis used them for their personal protection. Each family could keep one AK-47, Padilla told us. At the time, I thought that was perfectly ludicrous. I couldn't see the point of raiding houses if we allowed the very people who were supposed to be our enemies to continue to own automatic rifles. During my entire stay in Iraq, the rules about whether or not to take AK-47s from houses kept changing. One week we would be told to take every assault rifle we found. A little later, we would be instructed to let families keep a weapon for personal protection. Over time, I expected to find one gun in each house, and paid it no more attention than I would a television.

Other than weapons and people, the only things we found in our house raids were books, clothes, rugs, furniture and food. When we found money, jewellery or knives, we helped ourselves to them and to anything else that caught our fancy.

Not long into my stay in Iraq, I saw $100 in a house. I snapped up the US bills and stuffed them in my pocket. A man who was being zipcuffed and led out the door shouted back at me, angrily, 'Why are you taking that money? It's not yours.'

'This is American money,' I told him. 'You're not American, and you have no business having it.' The money stayed in my pocket.

Jewellery. Money. If it looked good, we helped ourselves.

I stole whatever I wanted in the first raids, but I stopped doing that after my first few weeks in Iraq. The more uneasy I felt about what we were doing there, the less I wanted to make matters worse.

Others in my platoon looted to their hearts' content. One fellow collected gold jewellery and mailed it home to his wife. Another lugged a television straight out of an Iraqi house. Others took ornate knives, and I saw one soldier make off with a beautiful rug. Who was going to stop us? We were the army of the United States of America, and we would do whatever we pleased.

Still I believed that eventually we would find the terrorists or the weapons that were said to be there, but it didn't take long before the raids left me feeling uncomfortable. It was easy to see the hatred in the eyes of the Iraqis as we broke apart their houses and arrested their men.

In the raids, I came to dislike the way Sergeant Jones loved to be the first one to bust into the homes. Jones, a freckled man from Ohio, had already done war duty in Afghanistan. He was just twenty-two, and I resented the fact that a man two years my junior outranked me in the squad. He had no wife or kids. He had been in the army for years, and talked about staying in it forever.

One of the things that upset me about Jones was what he had said to me in Fort Carson, Colorado, the day before we flew into war. He wanted to get my goat and he knew exactly how to mess me up. 'It's a known fact that your wife is gonna start fucking some other guy, the moment you're out of the country. You wait. You'll see. It happens to them all. By the time you're back, she will have stolen your money, served you divorce papers and found herself another man.'

I loved my wife to bits. Brandi and I already had three children, and I had never doubted her. But the seed of anxiety that Jones planted grew like a weed during my time in Iraq.

I thought of Brandi and of our children when Jones and I charged into civilians' houses. Jones had no family, but I did, and it tore me apart to terrorise families like that. We were finding no weapons of mass destruction or evidence of terrorism. I soon began to feel that breaking apart a house and terrorising its inhabitants was not something that should be done to any human being. Period.

One of the things that disturbed me the most in the house raids was having to run into bedrooms and round up sleeping Iraqi children. I couldn't help imagining how my own children would react if armed soldiers from another country burst into their rooms and tore them from bed. I was supposed to keep my guns trained on the children when I woke them, got them out of bed, and marched them outside. I couldn't do it, though. I could never point my M-249 at a child. I would tap them gently on the shoulder and the poor kids would leap from bed, petrified, screaming like the world was ending. And outside they would go, as their brothers and fathers were being zipcuffed and shoved onto the backs of trucks and sent out to who knows where.

■

Our first month in Ramadi—from the last days of April to about the end of May 2003—was the quietest and easiest of my time in Iraq. The people of Ramadi had been bombed before our arrival, so perhaps it took the Iraqi resistance some time to get organised. During our first tour of duty in Ramadi, we were not subjected to rocket or mortar attacks, nobody launched grenades at us, and almost nobody took shots at us as we moved about the city. Nobody in my platoon was injured or killed.

I fell into a pattern of four basic jobs: raiding homes; patrolling streets and traffic checkpoints; standing guard at banks, hospitals and military compounds; and doing grunt work where we had put up camp in Saddam Hussein's bombed-out palace.

Even back at the palace, we never got much sleep. Apache helicopters hovered and jets screamed at all times above us. At night, our forces shot constant illumination rounds into the sky. The rounds were like giant firecrackers, exploding one after the other so that darkness was never allowed to settle over Ramadi.

Sometimes I was ordered to patrol the banks of the Euphrates, located just a stone's throw from the palace. I would often see Iraqi fishermen in small boats, pulling the pins out of grenades and tossing them into the river. They would wait for the water to stop gushing up in fountains, and then they would scoop up all the dead fish. Eating fish full of shrapnel didn't seem like much of a meal to me, but the men were desperate for food and a livelihood.

I ran a pipe from the Euphrates to our palace and rigged up a pump so that the men in our platoon could use a make-shift shower. I also connected our electrical wires to the Iraqi power grid so that our lights, fans and air conditioners could run. I could have been electrocuted at any time, but I never stopped to worry about the dangers. I was living in constant fear of being attacked, was jacked up on adrenaline from all of the house raids, and was never allowed to sleep more than a couple of hours at a time. As a result I felt constantly stoned, and didn't think any more about the juice in the Iraqi power grid than I did about sleeping next to an American bomb or wandering out in the middle of the night to urinate next to an unexploded rocket-propelled grenade.

Because I was among the lowest-ranked, I got stuck every few days with one of the worst jobs going: to burn up all of our shit. We crapped into 50-gallon metal barrels, each sliced in half. When the barrels were full, I would toss in five gallons of diesel, light a match and use a fence post to stir the shit. Usually I would have two or three barrels burning at once, stirring each of them for hours at a time. I would have to keep tossing on more diesel and lighting more matches, and I had to keep stirring to make the shit burn. As I worked, the ashes settled all over my face and my hands. It took hours to burn down our shit in that way. In the first platoon of the 43rd Combat Engineer Company, I became the main shit burner, and I imagine that I stirred more of it than any soldier in Iraq.

In our quiet time, some of the men read or listened to

music. Most of them played GameBoys. Many times, we gathered together in groups to watch bootleg videos that we purchased from Iraqi street vendors or from Sayeed, a nineteen-year-old Iraqi who had studied in England and who was paid $20 a week to serve as our interpreter and errand boy.

On portable DVD players, we watched every kind of film imaginable. Action films. War movies. Porn. One time, Sayeed brought us a porn movie featuring Asian children. I looked in horror as a teenage girl in the video was tied on a stretcher and raped by two men. In the middle of a war zone, with tanks rolling and jets screaming, I stared numbly at the screen and asked myself what had gone wrong with the world. The other soldiers and I sat there stupidly and watched until Sergeant Lindsay broke up the show, called us all perverts, snatched the DVD and broke it with his hands.

Our commanders told us it was okay to masturbate, because they wanted us to check if we had any blood in our sperm—which, we were told, might suggest that we had ingested E. coli. For a laugh, some of the men began a competition to see who could go the longest without masturbating. We worked on the honour system, but it would have been hard to lie anyway.

Because I was eating with, crapping next to, sleeping beside and busting into homes with the same guys day in and day out, I ended up knowing them all pretty well. There's barely a thing about them I didn't know.

I knew whose wife has just written him a 'Dear John' letter, or, worse, told the poor guy who stood two hours in line to get to a phone that she had a new man in her bed. I knew who came from Indiana and who hailed from Alaska. I knew who liked video games and who read Dean Koontz novels. I knew which soldier had the biggest penis—measured by socket wrench, while the rest of us looked on—and who wanted to take a course in small engine repair when he got the hell out of Iraq. But one thing I almost never knew were the guys' first names. We all had our last name written on our uniforms, and our rank clearly marked, so everybody went by their last names. Nobody knew me as Josh. Nobody called me Josh. I was Key to one and all of them.

Because I grew up on a farm in Oklahoma and because I was five-foot-nine and weighed 215 pounds, I got called 'fat boy' more times than I care to remember, and I had to listen to a whole lot of nonsense about how people from Oklahoma fucked hogs.

My weight dropped fast in Iraq, however, and people stopped teasing me when they realised I was the quickest guy around when it came to using my hands. I can fix just about anything. And I can make just about any broken thing work. I may not fix it properly, but I'll fix it well enough to make it go again, and so they started calling me MacGyver again. Under orders, I jump-started Iraqi trucks, taxis and cars, and I hooked up our air conditioners to Iraqi electricity lines. By making myself useful, I kept the bullshit off my back and I managed to get along with most soldiers.

Specialist Sykora got it into his head to ask Sayeed, our interpreter, about how to make sexual taunts in Arabic. He and a bunch of others learned to say something like *sofeeni deeaytcha*, which was supposed to mean 'show me your tits', and *sofeeni goose goose*, which apparently meant 'show me your pussy'. On foot patrols he and a few others would shout the words at Iraqi women in the street. I never said those words, and I worried about the safety of the Iraqi women. Sometimes they were walking in the streets with their husbands. If their situation at home was anything like my mother's, I knew that their husbands would beat them just for having been taunted in this manner.

One day, while we were guarding the children's hospital in Ramadi, Jones—who also enjoyed taunting Iraqi women in the streets—stopped a woman doctor as she was entering the building. He made her remove her veil. I told Jones to leave her alone, but it was too late. She removed the veil and stared into Jones' face. In her eyes, I could see liquid fury. Later that day, as she was leaving, she passed us again and said to Jones: 'Actually, you asshole, I was born and raised in Boise, Idaho.' She went on to say that she had come to Iraq to help her people during the war. Jones was so embarrassed that he could not speak, and I was pleased for the woman from Idaho.

In the month of May, my platoon was ordered to go to the Ramadi police station to retrieve a truck full of rocket-propelled grenades and mortars. I was told that the truck contained one thousand rounds of live ammunition that had been taken from the Iraqis in battle. Escorted by our platoon, Iraqi police officers drove the truck full of ammunition to an isolated spot fifteen minutes outside the city, but we were ordered to wait for authorisation before blowing up the truck. In a display of typical army inefficiency, we left the truck unguarded in the desert and returned to Ramadi.

The next day, after receiving the detonation order, we returned to blow up the truck. It was gone. I shook my head in disgust. *Great work*, I thought. We just gave a thousand rounds of ammunition right back to the enemy.

After about a month in Iraq, the 43rd CEC was transferred out of Ramadi. We moved to Fallujah for a two-week period. One day in early June, not long into our stay in the new city, my platoon mates and I were standing guard outside a public building. Local Iraqi officials met there and held talks there with our own military commanders.

While standing at the back of the compound, I felt the ground shaking under a good thirty seconds of heavy gunfire. The barrage came from the other side of the building, which was being guarded by members of the 82nd Airborne Division. I heard voices crackling on army radios.

'What happened?' my squad leader asked.

'Looks like somebody got trigger happy,' somebody else said on the radio.

It was clear that once one soldier had started shooting, everybody else had joined in. A few minutes later, I saw about twelve body bags being carried away, and was told that the victims were all Iraqi civilians.

It was the first time I was aware of Iraqi civilians being

killed by American soldiers. I heard no more about the incident. I was struck by the absence of discussion in the aftermath. I kept my mouth shut too. Soldiers were not allowed to ask questions; to do so showed insubordination and invited punishment. I knew that for the slightest infraction, they could dock my pay and leave Brandi and the kids at home without any money coming in. In my presence, no soldiers or officers asked how or why the civilians came to be killed, and no explanations were offered. I came to see that silence usually followed in the wake of a killing.

One of my jobs in Fallujah and elsewhere was to monitor cars at traffic control points. We stopped cars, searched them and searched drivers. When we found people out driving after night-time curfews, we detained them and took their vehicles.

I hated it when people smiled at me at checkpoints. It made me want to punch them. What did they have to smile about? Did they know something I didn't know? Were they planning some sort of attack?

Early in my stay in Fallujah, while I was on checkpoint duty, one driver got out of his car and told me—in English—to go fuck myself. I felt an explosion of hatred and anger. I started beating the man. I was even tempted to shoot him. Something about all my pent-up anger and fear craved an explosion of violence in that very moment, but Lindsay—the sergeant first class who oversaw our platoon at the time—grabbed me and pulled me back.

'Lay off him, Key,' was all he said.

He didn't punish me, or say any more about it. I was angry

at the time, but not many minutes passed before I felt thankful that I had been stopped from seriously harming or killing the man.

I backed away from beating people at checkpoints, but saw that others continued to hand out beatings as often as they felt the urge.

While we were still doing traffic control in the first week of June in Fallujah, I saw Sergeant Lindsay join up with Specialist Mason to beat the daylights out of one man. My mouth fell open. Even Sergeant Lindsay was losing it now. I saw the beating, but had no idea what had provoked it. Maybe the man had said the wrong thing, or smiled the wrong way. One thing was clear: he hadn't attempted any sort of assault or attack.

In my countless days at traffic control points, I never once saw an Iraqi civilian threaten or harm an American soldier. Lindsay and Mason kicked the man in the back and the head and kept on kicking once he fell down. They rubbed his face in the sand and then began spitting on him. I remember thinking that it was going way too far, but I knew I didn't have the rank to stop the attack. Finally, an Abrams tank belonging to another platoon stopped and a sergeant jumped out.

'What the hell are you doing?' the sergeant asked, telling Mason to get away from the man and to stand behind the tank.

Lindsay told the sergeant to mind his own business. 'My troops will do whatever I tell them to do,' he said.

The tank sergeant did not outrank Lindsay, so he got back inside and drove on. But Lindsay and Mason did not return to their beating. They let the man get up, climb into his car and drive away. We never discussed the incident in our platoon. It was not that far out of the ordinary.

Every day or two, I saw American troops beating Iraqi civilians. In our own platoon, all we had to do was look at our highest-ranking sergeant to see that it was okay to kick and punch Iraqis whenever we felt the urge. Fortunately, I no longer felt the urge. I also knew that I was powerless to stop somebody like Sergeant Lindsay from punching an Iraqi civilian. If I had spoken directly to him about it, I would have been violating the chain of command. I wasn't even authorised to speak to a superior officer unless he addressed me first. If I saw something that concerned me in Sergeant Lindsay's behaviour, the only course of action—apart from keeping my mouth shut—would have been to speak to my team leader, who, if he felt like it, would have had to speak to his squad leader, who, in turn and if so inclined, would have had to go to Lindsay himself. For all that, I was sure, I would have been bawled out for leaving my post and likely docked some pay. The simplest thing to do was keep my own mouth shut and stay out of trouble. So that is what I did.

◼

The people of Fallujah were so accustomed to bullets flying that some of them walked about oblivious to the dangers. It was as if they felt that their lives were so entirely in the hands of God it would be useless to even bother ducking for cover.

One day, I was with my squad mates on our APC, chasing a truck. Somebody had said that shots had been fired at us from the truck. As it drove and we gave chase over a bridge, my squad leader—Sergeant Padilla—sat on top of our APC, blasting away with his 50-calibre machine gun. Perched as usual on top of our vehicle, I could see an old man walking towards us. Bullets whistled past him, blasting chips out of concrete walls on the side of the bridge, but the old man kept walking calmly, as if in a dream. I thought it was a miracle that he was not hit, but he didn't even appear to be thinking about it.

Unfortunately, the violence meted out by American troops was not limited to kicking and punching.

One day in our first week in Fallujah, my entire platoon—three squads, consisting of a total of about twenty men—was stationed at a traffic control point. Lieutenant Joyce was the highest-ranking officer with us that day. While the other two squads monitored approaching cars, I was busy with my squad mates searching vehicles and drivers. While I was looking under the hood of a car, checking for bombs and hidden weapons, the ground started to shake. I dropped to my knees, but realised that it was fire from my own troops. The hail of gunfire came from M-16 rifles, M-249s, and 50-calibre machine guns. Even a Bradley tank got into the act. The fire was coming from the first and second squads of my platoon, and I could see that they were firing at a white car with yellow stripes that had two people inside.

The car had driven too close to the checkpoint, about ten feet past the line at which it was supposed to stop. As a result, it had been brought to a halt in the most murderous way. When the car stopped inching forward and the gunfire ceased, my squad mates and I ran to the vehicle. We found it riddled with five-inch holes. Inside the car, one man was dead. His head was only attached by a few threads of flesh to his neck, and blood was splattered all over him and the car. Nobody touched him. But then I saw a boy in the front seat. He looked like he was about ten years old. A medic pulled him out. One of the boy's arms was nearly severed, but he was alive. The boy was conscious, and he was looking at his father. With the help of the medic, we threw the boy in our APC, raced him to the Ramadi hospital and dropped him off there.

When we got back to the checkpoint, I spent ten minutes searching the vehicle and patting down the dead man. There were no weapons inside it. There was nothing unusual in the car, except all the blood that we had made run.

About twenty minutes later, Lieutenant Joyce got off his army radio and told us all to pack up and leave. We left the car and the driver right where they were, in the middle of busy road. I couldn't stop thinking about how we didn't even put the man in a body bag and take him to the hospital or to our compound, where his family would know to find him.

When we got back to our compound, I vomited. Sykora and Mason also threw up. I had never before seen a man shot to death. As far as I could tell, he was killed simply because he hadn't known where to stop his car.

The next day, as I was stationed on top of our moving APC, I looked out at the spot where the man had been killed. He and his car were gone.

■

In Fallujah, we stayed in a compound of bungalows outside the city. In my own mind, I called it Dreamland, its artificial lake seemed so utterly removed from our day-to-day activities at war in Iraq. In our free time, we tried to forget our troubles and the shooting we had seen by jumping off a 60-foot bridge, straight into the water. Lewis didn't want to jump, so we just pushed him off the side of the bridge. Even Sykora, who could barely swim, was forced into the water, and I watched as he dog-paddled back to the edge.

A few days after we had left the dead man in his bullet-ridden car, the violence began again.

After nightfall, our platoon left Dreamland to drive across Fallujah to a traffic control point. I rode as usual on top of the APC, holding my M-249 rifle. Sergeant Padilla sat up in front of me, on his turreted 50-calibre machine gun. Specialist Mason was driving. Two APCs belonging to the other squads rode directly ahead of us, and behind us travelled an Abrams tank.

As we approached an intersection, I saw a small white pick-up truck driving in our direction. It looked like a Toyota or a Nissan. It made a quick left-hand turn, cutting in front of us. This split us off from the second APC, but I saw no sign of danger and there were about thirty yards to spare.

Nonetheless, Padilla let loose with his 50-calibre machine gun. Blasting away with bullets about six inches long, he shot the car and brought it to a halt. I saw a trail of gas leaking from the car. Padilla shifted his gun, aimed at the trail of gas and shot again. The line of gas caught fire and flew back towards the truck. When it hit the gas tank, the truck exploded in a ball of fire.

We kept on driving. I looked back at the explosion and the fire. I watched our Abrams tank roll right through it and keep following us. It looked like something straight out of *Rambo*. The boys in my squad let out some hollers of delight.

'Man, did you see that?' someone called out.

'Did you see that tank run right over that thing?' said another.

I didn't see any reason for Padilla to shoot up the truck. It had enough room to turn without causing an accident. I said nothing, but later that night, I heard Padilla tell Sergeant Lund, who was asking questions, 'What if the truck was cutting us off?' From what I could see, the truck hadn't been shot because it posed a danger to us. It had been shot merely because it had annoyed my staff sergeant. The truck could have been stopped, or even confiscated. But it was quicker and less trouble all around to simply shoot until it exploded, and blow its driver and passengers—if there were any—to bits.

Only six weeks had passed since my arrival in Iraq, but I could already see that for American soldiers at war, it had become too easy to shoot and too easy to kill. We couldn't catch or see the real insurgents, let alone take a clear shot at them, so civilians would have to do.

In two short weeks in Fallujah, I had already heard gunfire from another division bring down twelve civilians and I had witnessed my own platoon members killing at least two others. I had already seen more blood and death than I cared for, and I felt that we were wrong to be dishing out such violence against civilians. Still, I thought that our military presence was justified in Iraq. I still believed that we were there to eradicate terrorism, but that the villains had simply not yet shown their faces. Sooner or later, I thought, we would catch them. In the meantime, my job was to follow orders: stand guard, raid houses and stir shit. I did what I was told and kept my mouth shut.

# FOUR

# RETURN TO RAMADI

**D**uring my first tour of duty in Ramadi, I had no way of
knowing that it would be my quietest time in Iraq.

Camped so close to the Euphrates River, my squad mates
and I stripped down to our underwear one hot afternoon and
jumped in the water. We felt carefree for a while and in no
real danger, even with our weapons set aside, so we shouted
and laughed and dunked each other under the water until we
saw things floating past us. They were dull green, and cube-
shaped. Each side was about six inches long. Unexploded
mines. I had learned about them in military training. If any

one of them had blown up, the Euphrates River would have become our instant grave. We swam to the shore, climbed onto the bank, got back in our gear and never again jumped into the Euphrates.

About a month later, when we returned to the city after spending two weeks in Fallujah, Ramadi had changed for the worse. It had now become the war zone I had first anticipated when arriving in Iraq, with one exception—the enemy was never visible.

Almost every night, I could hear the mortars being lobbed towards the former Iraqi military compound that my 43rd Combat Engineer Company had moved into, for lodgings.

The most frightening thing about being mortared was watching the flying bombs become a little more accurate each time. A mortar comes in different sizes, but some of those hurtling towards us were the size of a football, with little wings on them. I thought of them as long bombs, lobbed by Iraqi quarterbacks who walked just a little closer to us each time they let one go. Clearly, the Iraqi fighters had people stationed close by, given how close the mortars were coming to their targets—us. The second round would come a little closer, and the third round even closer; we described this as the Iraqis 'walking the mortars in on us'. Wherever they were—and we could never see them—they were moving their launchers a little closer.

Initially, the mortars were terrifying. Sometimes I could make out a faint whir as they sailed through the air. We called it a 'splash' when the mortar exploded, and the kill zone had a radius of some thirty yards. The small, falling bombs kept us jittery and on our nerves. None of them was big enough to blow up a building, but any one of them, if it landed close enough, could kill us in a second.

Eventually, I learned to sleep through at least some mortar attacks, but not everybody was so lucky. Sergeant Fadinetz, for example, a divorced, thick-set man in his mid-thirties who had been in the military for years and had served overseas in South Korea, tried to talk a good game during the day. Sometimes he would lift up his chin and say, 'Key, I never want to see you or any of the other sons of bitches in this company once we get out of this war and go home. Once I'm a civilian, as far as I'm concerned, you guys are history. Don't come looking for me, because I won't want to see you.'

But Fadinetz wasn't as tough as he sounded. He rode with me on top of our APC, told me that he was from Rochester and hoped to go to college one day in Colorado, and I sensed that it took a certain effort for him not to complain about the madness of our assignments.

You get to know the guys you go to war with, and Fadinetz's fears would come out at night, when the mortars landed and he woke up screaming. I could only imagine the way the sounds of war must have twisted his dreams into nightmares, and I felt for the man as I watched him wake up in terror beside me. Honestly, I didn't know what was worse for him: the nightmares, or waking to the sounds of explosions little more than a kill zone away.

Adrenaline jolted through your system like an electric

shock, and woke you completely—even if you had been sound asleep, and had only had an hour of shut-eye in the last day.

It was a strange way to fight a war. We never saw the people who shot at us, never spotted the mortar launchers, and never located the people who used rockets to propel grenades at us. Because our enemy remained invisible, our fears and frustrations mounted, but we could always take our frustrations out on the civilians.

The duty that frightened me the most in Iraq, was to go out with my platoon on foot patrols. We frequently patrolled the streets of Ramadi, trying to engage the enemy, hoping to lure somebody into a fire fight. Fortunately for us, the most common thing that happened on our foot patrols was also the worst: once in a while, a man or a child would throw a rock at us. Still, I felt completely vulnerable in those moments. I couldn't stop thinking about the warnings I had heard during my training: Iraqis were Muslims and Muslims were terrorists and they were all out to kill Americans.

In the thick crowds of people, sometimes I would catch sight of a grenade riding on the tip of a weapon perched on an Iraqi's shoulder. At any moment, I feared, someone would lob a grenade at us, take a clean shot from a rooftop or even shove a knife into me while we were making our way through the crowded markets.

Now that we were back for our second tour of duty in the city, few people were still smiling at us, and a number made no effort to mask their hatred. One day, when a butcher in the market caught me looking at him, he raised his knife and held the sharp edge close to his own throat as I walked by. I swept the rooftops with my eyes, keeping my weapon ready in case I pinpointed a sniper.

Our foot patrols often went on for hours, and took place in sweltering heat. Some days in July, I would estimate that the temperature exceeded 120 degrees. The breeze provided no relief at all; it felt like a blowdryer smacking me in the face. Between the uniform, backpack and the M-247, I carried one hundred extra pounds with each step, and I would finish the patrols soaked in sweat.

Some of the men struggled gravely in the heat. Specialist Sykora became so dehydrated during one long foot patrol that he began to rock back and forth on his heels, like a boxer caught on the chin, and then crumpled to the ground. We surrounded him to keep him safe and radioed for backup. A humvee rolled up within minutes. We carried him out to it. He recovered quickly after a medic hooked him up to an intravenous unit.

One day, my platoon mates and I were walking single file through a crowded Ramadi market. Thousands of people were milling about, and I simply could not stop thinking about the warnings issued by my superiors: the Iraqis were Muslims, and Muslims were terrorists, and therefore I was at risk of attack at any moment. The fruit and the meat stalls were close on either side, and with all of the market-goers it was hard to stay in contact with the soldier walking in front of me in our single file. Suddenly, an Iraqi man cut in front of me, separating me from the soldier ahead of me. I feared he would try to plunge a knife into me, so I slugged him in the face, pushed by as he stumbled and ran forward to join my comrades.

It was always with relief that I made it back to the compound at the end of the day. During our second tour of duty in Ramadi, we no longer camped in Saddam Hussein's bombed-out palace. This time, my entire 43rd Combat Engineer Company took over a former Iraqi military compound consisting of several bungalow buildings. The compound was located close to the Euphrates River, in central Ramadi. Like most buildings we occupied in Iraqi, it had been bombed earlier by our own forces.

When we moved into the compound, we discovered an Iraqi family of thirteen people—a man with three wives and nine children—inhabiting the facility. I assumed that their own home had been destroyed by American bombs. They had been squatting there with their clothes, pots and pans, blankets and all their other possessions. The husband reacted wildly when we commandeered his home. Clearly, he was about to lose the little security that his family had. He shouted at Sayeed, our interpreter, who relayed the message to Captain Conde, who led our company. At the time, I happened to be standing about ten feet away with Sergeant Padilla so I was close enough to hear Captain Conde laugh and tell the man, 'You've got two hours to get out of here.' The man had no choice but to pack up his things and leave with his family.

On other occasions, distraught Iraqis came to us at the compound. While I stood guard, a man came with his wife and daughter and complained that his daughter had just been raped. I was not able to tell if they were complaining that Americans or Iraqis had committed the crime. I radioed my commander for instructions and was told to send the man off because we couldn't get involved in people's domestic affairs.

Another time, a man complained that one of our illumination rounds had crashed into his home and burned up his bed. I thought my superiors would send him packing, but he was given a small amount of American cash—about $50, I believe—and I heard talk among my platoon mates that my officers had a small fund to soothe Iraqis with minor grievances.

As we resumed our regular duties in Ramadi—patrolling streets, checking traffic, guarding buildings and raiding homes—we began to receive nightly reports from our commanders. When my six squad mates were all gathered together at night, our leader—Sergeant Padilla—would usually read out official army notices. They often contained news items about American soldiers recently killed in Iraq. I thought of these notices as haunting bedtime stories that made all of us more nervous about our own safety as mortars fell and rocket-propelled grenades exploded closer and closer to us.

Just two months earlier, President George W. Bush had flown to the aircraft carrier USS *Abraham Lincoln*, off the coast of San Diego, to give his 'mission accomplished' speech.

In Iraq, we had heard about the speech. 'In the Battle of Iraq, the United States and our allies have prevailed,' the president had said. As I listened to the sound of gunfire and explosions, I wished it were true.

During our house raids and at our traffic control points, we continued to find grenades and AK-47 assault rifles in homes and in cars. We confiscated all grenades that we found, but we only took the AK-47s when we felt like it or when we were instructed to do so—which was perhaps half the time.

Not long into our second tour of duty in Ramadi, I was working at a traffic control point, pulling over vehicles. The standard practice was to order everybody out of the car, and to have the driver open the hood and the trunk. A black, four-door Mercedes Benz pulled up: the driver had three adult male passengers. Glancing inside the car, I spotted four grenades tucked between the two front seats.

The driver was a young man, and he didn't say or do anything to provoke me. However, the mere presence of those grenades set off my anger. I hauled him from the car and began kicking and punching him. An older man in the car began screaming at me in Arabic. I couldn't understand a word he said, and he would not shut up, so I beat him badly too.

By the time I finished with them, both men were bleeding profusely. With the help of my squad mates, I zipcuffed the men, threw one of them in the trunk and stuffed the other three in the back seat.

Sergeant Fadinetz got into the passenger seat, I jumped into the front, and we drove through Ramadi for ten minutes to the police station, where we turned over the men for arrest. I have no idea what became of them, but I do know what happened to their car: I stole it for my squad to use. We had no keys, so I hot-wired it and attached a switch to make it easy for my squad mates to start. We used the Mercedes on our house raids, preferring to arrive in an unmarked vehicle to disguise our approach.

When I beat up the two men, I justified it to myself on the grounds that that they had grenades in the car. But the truth was that grenades were everyday items in Iraq, just like the rifles we routinely left behind on our house raids, and I had no good reason to attack the men.

My own moral judgment in Iraq was disintegrating under the pressure of being a soldier, feeling vulnerable and having no clear enemy to kill. We were encouraged to beat up on the enemy, and, given the absence of any real enemy, we picked our fights with civilians who were powerless to resist. We knew that we would not have to account for our actions. Because we were fearful, sleep-deprived and jacked up on caffeine, adrenaline and testosterone, and because our officers constantly reminded us that all Iraqis were our enemies, civilians included, it was tempting to steal, no big deal to punch, and easy to kill.

We were Americans in Iraq, and we could do anything we wanted to do.

At this time, I was still stealing money, knives and sunglasses from cars and houses. One time, I found 1.5 million dinars in an Iraqi truck that I had been assigned to drive to a hospital, and I took that money too. I was not sure how much the money was worth, but I imagined about $500. It paid for my cigarettes and Coca-Cola for a while. But one day at a traffic checkpoint, when a man with a large family complained about having no job and no family, I tossed the rest of the money in his back seat and sent him on his way.

Another time, I made a man at a traffic control point remove his artificial leg. Inside it, I found $10,000 in $100 bills. I know it was $10,000, because I counted every bill. If my superiors had not been present, I would have considered stuffing it in my pockets and sending it home. But I was flanked by my superior, Sergeant Gurillo, and I gave him the money when I had finished counting. He handed it to his superior, Captain Bower. I have no idea what happened to the money, but the man with the false leg was carrying on angrily in Arabic, and I doubt very much that he ever got it back.

I am not proud of the things that I did in Iraq. But before my company left Ramadi near the end of July, I stopped beating civilians and stopped stealing from them, and I did it no more for the rest of my time in the country. But as my conscience began to catch up with me, I witnessed American soldiers and officers losing control of themselves more and more often.

Not long after I beat up the men with the grenades, I found myself yet again at a traffic control point. This time it was late in the evening, and we had decided to stop all vehicles that were out past our night-time curfew of about 10 pm. For an hour or two, we stopped about forty taxis and forced the drivers to get out of their vehicles. To their distress, we told them that we were detaining them for breaking the curfew. While some laughed defiantly and others swore, we assembled all the drivers and herded them in small groups into the back of a five-ton truck. My platoon mates began driving them down to the Ramadi police station, where they were arrested. My superiors instructed me to remain behind and hotwire the taxis so that the rest of my platoon mates could race them to the police station. One of the captains who commanded our company jumped in a taxi and raced with us.

For an hour or two that night, my platoon mates had the time of their lives. They bumped and banged their vehicles through the city, but nobody cared. Nobody, that is, in a position to do something about it. I got into the last taxi and got my turn, cranking it up to over 60 miles per hour as I raced through the streets of Ramadi.

We found various other ways to amuse ourselves during quiet moments at the compound. Once again, I earned a few brownie points by hooking up air conditioning units to the Iraqi power lines.

We were supposed to sleep on cots on the main floor, but even with the air conditioners, only a small part of the compound was cool enough to sleep. I often went up to the roof to catch some of the evening breeze. Using cinder blocks and an iron bar, I started weightlifting. We would hook up portable DVD players to our APC, huddle close together and watch bootleg movies from our stash such as *Hawk* and *House of a Thousand Corpses*.

In my downtime, I chainsmoked, swapped cigarettes with my buddy Private Ricky Connor—a twenty-three-year-old single man from Amarillo, Texas—and teased him mercilessly about how the Oklahoma University Sooners football team spanked his Texas Longhorns team 73–21. We were not allowed to have satellite telephones, but some platoon mates kept them anyway, and one of them was able to tell us football scores twenty-four hours after the games had ended. Connor was a patriotic American who believed, and seemed to keep on believing, that America was doing the right thing in Iraq. Despite my doubts about the big picture, I liked hanging out with him to talk about Oklahoma and Texas.

We needed to relax to hang onto our sanity in an increasingly punishing environment. We rarely slept more than two hours at a time, and frequently stood guard and conducted other duties for more than twenty-four hours consecutively.

At least once a week, officers told us that we were in grave danger of attack. In Fallujah, for example, the soldiers in my company were made to wait in armoured vehicles outside a walled compound of old, bombed-out Iraqi military buildings. We were told that 10,000 Iranian sympathisers of Saddam Hussein had congregated inside. They were planning to riot, we were told, and we had to be ready for battle. It seemed like a ridiculous story, but I had no choice but to join my fellow soldiers in surrounding the compound. We stood outside it for hours, while aircraft screamed overheard, Apache helicopters hovered and Abrams tanks rolled into play. Finally, after hours of waiting and repeated warnings that we were in danger of a riot, the doors were opened. About one hundred unarmed women were let out. There had been no rioters, no weapons, no sympathisers of Saddam Hussein who had miraculously appeared from Iran, and no threat to our safety.

I believe that the repeated warnings of danger were meant to keep us off guard, and to keep us frightened enough to do exactly what we were told. But what I witnessed was that after a month or two in Iraq, the other soldiers and I could not help but take the warnings less and less seriously, like they were coming from the boy who cried wolf.

Still, somebody, somewhere, was trying to kill us. We couldn't see them, but they were there. A man named Sergeant Taylor, who worked with another platoon in my company, was driving across Ramadi in a humvee when a bomb blew up under the vehicle. My squad mates and I had been guarding a bank at the time, and we were ordered to race across Ramadi in our APC to help out. We found Sergeant Taylor—who was already overdue to return back home to the States—with an eye hanging out of his face and with shrapnel wounds across his body. He was evacuated for medical care, and as far as I know, he lived.

The next night, we were told to raid houses in a specific neighbourhood for the attack on the humvee. One of my sergeants said, 'Tonight it's retaliation time against the City of Ramadi.'

We carried on with our house raids, ransacking houses and detaining every man we could find.

A short time later, Staff Sergeant Padilla woke me up at about 1 am to tell me to climb out of my sleeping bag and get ready for action. Our platoon was designated a Quick Reaction Force, and our orders were to rush to help out Americans soldiers from the 124th Infantry Division who were said to be caught in a fire fight with hundreds of Iraqis. I did not believe the story. I had yet to see one Iraqi militant rioting and shooting, so it seemed unlikely that I would now find 300 doing so.

My six squad mates and I jumped in our APC and I took my usual position on top left of the vehicle, training my machine gun on rooftops as we drove in formation with the other two APCs in our platoon.

I rode up top with Sergeant Fadinetz and Staff Sergeant Padilla. Down below, Specialist Mason drove while Sergeant Jones, Specialist Sykora and Private Lewis sat with him. Sergeant Jones shouted that we were on our way to face hundreds of rioting Iraqis in an alley. Up top, Sergeant Fadinetz and I shared a private laugh over this—we both felt it was highly unlikely.

We rode slowly for about ten minutes. We made two turns in our APC and while moving just a few miles an hour, travelled towards the banks of the Euphrates River, along a small road that we called 'the red route'. Sergeant Padilla and I could make out the sounds of a fire fight.

It was about 2 am, but I could see very well because there

were streetlights on our road, and because of the American illumination rounds that kept the sky lit up all night.

Suddenly, I looked over to my left and saw the bodies of four decapitated Iraqis in their bloodied white robes, lying a few feet from a bullet-ridden pickup truck to the side of the road. Because I sat on the top left of the vehicle, and because the bodies were on the left-hand side of the road, I had them in clear view. I assumed that someone had used a massive amount of gunfire to behead them.

'Shit,' I said.

A few seconds later, our slow-moving APC came to a stop. Among the three APCs in our convoy, I was the only soldier immediately ordered down to the ground. As I slid down into the vehicle and then out the hatch, Sergeant Jones told me to look for brass casings, which would be signs that Iraqi fighters with AK-47s had been shooting at American soldiers in the area.

I saw no brass casings, but I did see an American soldier shouting at the top of his lungs at two other soldiers who stood next to him.

'We fucking lost it, we just fucking lost it!' the soldier was shouting. He was in a state of complete distress, but the soldiers next to him were not reacting. The distressed soldier stood about twenty yards from me, and another forty or so yards from the four bodies.

I did not know whom he was hollering at, so I turned. Two other soldiers were laughing and kicking the heads of the decapitated Iraqis. It was clearly a moment of amusement, for them. This was their twisted game of soccer.

I froze at the sight, and for a moment could not believe my eyes. But I saw what I saw, and was so revolted and horrified that I defied Sergeant Jones' orders and climbed right back into the APC.

'I'm not having anything to do with that,' I said. I wondered who the soldiers could possibly be, what their rank was and who was their commanding officer, but I had not see, any details in the brief time I was on the ground.

Sergeant Jones looked at me like I was crazy for defying him, but I was not sure if he had seen what I had seen. I doubted it, because he was stuck inside the APC, which was facing the opposite direction.

On the radio, Lieutenant Joyce—who was in one of the other APCs—asked Sergeant Padilla why I had got back in my vehicle, but I was too shocked to offer an answer. I just climbed back to my spot on top of the APC and—like my fellow soldiers—faced the opposite direction to where the bodies and the heads were. We were still supposedly protecting the American soldiers on the ground from attack.

We remained in that one spot for another thirty or forty minutes, holding our position, facing down an alley, preparing for the promised onslaught of rioting Iraqis. They never came.

As far as I could see, the only armed men in the area were American soldiers from the 124th Infantry Division and from my own 43rd Combat Engineer Company. Finally, we spun around 180 degrees to return to the compound. As we began to roll, I could see again the four decapitated bodies as well as the shot-up truck, but I could not see the heads.

Our APC moved slowly forward, but suddenly swerved so sharply that I nearly lost my balance up top. I had no idea why Mason, who was driving, had made us swerve like that.

Later, I asked Specialist Sykora if he had seen what I had seen. He said nothing at all, but just looked through me with the thousand-mile stare, a sort of trance that made him appear to be looking off into space.

The compound, when we returned to it, seemed even less safe to me than before. It had been bombed, like most of the other military buildings and palaces, before we moved in, and I couldn't sleep in it or walk through it without having bits of concrete and dust fall on my head. I stood guard duty for a few hours, and as I was finishing, went to our urinals to relieve myself. There, I found myself standing beside Mason, our APC driver, who was about to begin guard duty.

'Hey, man, you nearly made me fall off the APC,' I said. 'Why the hell did you swerve like that?'

'I was trying to run over one of the heads,' he said.

'You've gone right fucking nuts,' I told him.

Mason threw me a furious look, and our conversation went no further.

The killing of the four Iraqis, the games American soldiers played with their heads, the silence of my own military commanders when we came upon the scene, and Mason's attempt to join in on the act all combined to snap the last threads of belief that I had in my country and what it was doing at war. I had always seen my fellow Americans as upholders of justice in the world, but now I had come face to face with the gross indecency of our actions in Iraq.

Later that morning I asked Sergeant Skillings about the soldiers who had been out with us at the Euphrates, and he confirmed that they belonged to the Florida National Guard, part of the 124th Infantry Division. I hoped that someone would write a report about the night's events, and I naively asked Staff Sergeant Padilla if I could see it. He told me that it was none of my damn business and that I should leave it alone. I had expected such an answer, but had not been able to prevent myself from asking the question in the first place. It was too horrendous an act to be left unreported, but Padilla's response led me to suspect that my commanding officers would not write a single word about the incident.

I didn't raise the matter again, but the event changed the way I thought about my army in this war.

I didn't know much about the Geneva Conventions, but I knew one thing: what I had witnessed was grossly wrong.

We were soldiers of the American army. In Iraq, we were supposed to be stomping out terrorism, bringing democracy and acting as a force for good in the world. Instead, we had become monsters in a residential neighbourhood. Civilians in houses just fifty yards away could easily have been watching as soldiers in the American army not only shot dead four civilians, but used the outrageous amount of gunfire necessary to cut their heads off. I didn't have to be a lawyer to know that armies at war were not supposed to rape, plunder, loot or pillage. They were not supposed to harm civilians, or mutilate the bodies of the dead. I was so troubled that I could not speak about the incident.

My grandparents were far from a perfect people, but I had learned one or two fundamental lessons growing up on their farm. It was wrong to attack defenceless people. And if you did get into a fist fight, it would be utterly despicable to start kicking your opponent once he was down.

When I was back home in Oklahoma, if somebody had described the situation of the decapitated corpses, I would have had a hard time believing it. I would not have wanted to accept that American soldiers would behave in this way over-seas. But I was no longer in Oklahoma, and I could not deny what my eyes had seen. American soldiers had become the enemy in Iraq. We were bringing hate to the people of Iraq; as a result, the Iraqis would hate us for generations to come.

I was unable to forget the scene of the decapitated bodies and the heads kicked by American soldiers. Sometimes, in my dreams, decapitated heads plagued me with accusations. They told me what I was slowly realising: the American military had betrayed the values of my country. We had become a force for evil, and I could not escape the fact that I was part of the machine.

# FIVE

# THE GIRL AT THE
# HOSPITAL

Specialist Sykora was hooked on Dean Koontz novels, '007' and 'Splinter Cell' on his GameBoy, and World Wrestling Federation matches. He was originally from Chicago, but his wife and children lived in Ohio. He said his wife would not let him leave the military because they needed the salary and the health insurance benefits. He hoped to change his life one day and learn how to repair small engines, but he he was already thirty-six. In the army world, I wondered if he had become a lifer.

Not long after the four Iraqi civilians were shot and beheaded, Sykora and I decided to get drunk. There were strict rules against drinking while we were at war but we took a chance anyway, trying to drown our anxieties in six 20-ounce beers and a bottle of Jordanian whisky.

We were in shock over the deaths, but we were also worked up over Captain Bower, who had recently taken over command of our company. Bower was tall, thin and wore glasses. He had a direct and forceful personality, and I didn't like him. Bower knew that his soldiers had been complaining about day-to-day dangers and he addressed the matter head-on in a meeting of our platoon. He poked me in the chest and at the same time began lecturing Sergeant Fadinetz.

'You know what, Sergeant?' he said. 'Your dangers don't matter to me. If one hundred of you walk out that door, as long as 75 per cent of you walk back inside, I'm a happy man because it's an acceptable fatality rate.'

Sykora and I got the message then and there that we were little more than numbers in the eyes of our superiors. We felt that it didn't really matter to our commanders whether we lived or died.

Feeling that we were expendable commodities gave Sykora and me all the more to complain about as we sought shelter in an isolated part of the compound—an area that nobody was supposed to enter, because our own air force had bombed it so thoroughly that nobody knew when the entire structure would fall in—and downed our beer and whisky.

Food was another source of distraction to us. Two black

men in my company refused to eat the military rations, and instead used their pocket money to buy lamb sandwiches daily at $2 a pop. I liked those sandwiches too and ate a few of them, smothered in Tabasco sauce and ketchup. They came straight from an Iraqi vendor who cooked large legs of lamb over a rotisserie fire by the side of the road.

Even as we broke into their houses, patrolled their streets and stopped their cars, Iraqi vendors kept coming at us. They sold clothing, pipes and cigarettes. They sold kebabs, Coke and ice. They sold porn videos. They sold bootleg movies shot on hand-held cameras inside movie theatres. Our food was so bad and we were so bored that we kept those vendors in business. I spent about $50 a month on food, drinks and souvenirs from street vendors. Some of the guys in my platoon spent more.

One man in my company—a bone-thin nineteen-year-old named Private Lewis—had a mom back in Illinois who made the best damn beef jerky in the world. Hot and spicy, it lit a fire at the back of my throat. Whenever Lewis received care packages from home, I received a big wad of beef jerky and stretched it out as long as I could.

For most of us, however, there was no getting around our staple food—the military rations called Meals Ready to Eat, or MREs for short. We were supposed to eat three of them a day. Most soldiers agreed that the MREs were among the grossest foods known to man. In its almost indestructible package, the dried food was said to last up ten years. For a soldier at war, the food was mostly about convenience: an

MRE actually heats itself up. You stick a package inside a pouch, add a bit of water, and the stuff starts bubbling and boiling on its own. You have a hot meal in a minute or two— but that didn't mean we thought they were edible. I made up my own nicknames—*Beef Screw* (Beef Stew), *Please Relieve Me* (Cheese Tortellini), *Stork Piss* (Pork Rib) and *Gun Powder* (Clam Chowder).

I could stomach just one of the MREs, and I let my squad mates know that no man's life was safe if he took it. The Beef Enchilada was mine and mine only. When I drowned it in Tabasco sauce, it reminded me vaguely of Mexican food in Oklahoma. Apart from bringing back, faintly, the taste of home, the Beef Enchilada had one other advantage: it wasn't ruined by the presence of vegetables. I'm not your vegetable sort of guy. As far as I'm concerned, vegetables are what food eats.

When my squad mates and I travelled in our armoured personnel carrier to do guard duty at the Ramadi children's hospital, we took our MREs along with us. Because our shifts usually lasted for twenty-four hours, we kept a stash of MREs in the APC parked outside the hospital. While changing posts at the hospital every four or so hours, I was free to grab an MRE and a bottle of water.

Guard duty at the hospital was mentally draining. There was always the threat of danger, so we were required to have our weapons locked and ready to fire. However, nothing ever seemed to happen, which made the days go by slowly. When the sun beat down on us, it was hard to find an inch of shade.

Sometimes, while standing guard on the roof, I would chat with a middle-aged doctor named Muhammad who came outside on his breaks to smoke cigarettes and look out over the city. He spoke English well, asked about my own family and told me that he had seventeen children. One day, while he fiddled with the stethoscope around his neck, he said that two of his sons had been hanged in Ramadi by Saddam Hussein's men. He didn't care for Saddam Hussein, but he didn't like having Americans in the city either.

'Where are you from?' he said.

I told him a little about life in Oklahoma. Like many Iraqis, he seemed stunned to hear that I had grown up poor. But he was heartened to hear that I had a wife and three sons.

'So when do you think the US troops will pull out?' he said.

'I have no idea,' I replied, 'but I've got a feeling we're going to be here for a long, long time.'

He grimaced.

'I've got to tell you,' I continued, 'I'm looking forward to getting out of here just as much as you would like to see me gone.'

He laughed at that. I asked what he had been doing before the war began, and he said that he had taught medicine at universities in Ramadi and Baghdad. I had heard talk about how difficult it was for Iraqi hospitals to get medical supplies after the first Persian Gulf War, and was going to ask him about that, but an angry voice crackled on my walkie-talkie. It was one of my superiors.

'Key! Get away from that man and stop fraternising with the enemy.'

Muhammad came back at other times, though, and we had other moments to exchange a few words. He liked his cigarettes, and we had that in common.

'What do you do in Oklahoma?'

'Whatever jobs I can find,' I said. 'Painting, delivering pizza, but welding is what I really want to do.'

'My country could use a few welders,' he said.

'Over here, this is just a job for me, and it's not making any sense to me either.'

'A job?' he said, giving me a puzzled look. 'You're different from most of the Americans here.'

The next time we met outside the hospital, Muhammad gave me a small edition of the Qur'an. It was in Arabic, but I was touched by the gift. Before any of my superiors could notice, I slid the book quickly into my trouser pocket.

'I hope this will help you,' he said, 'and that you will return home safely to the ones who love you.'

◼

I thought of Muhammad, and of how difficult his job must be, each time I walked through the hospital corridors and up the stairs to the roof, where I sometimes stood guard.

The trips were depressing. I shuddered at the thought of needing treatment in such a filthy place. Needles were scattered all over the floors, and by toilets I saw blood and foetuses. I imagined that the tiny, half-formed bodies had come from miscarriages, and stopped to think about how hard the war had to be on the women of Iraq. Given that the hospital lacked the equipment to properly dispose of needles and foetuses, it gave me the shivers imagining the conditions in which the living were treated. I wondered to what degree our occupation of the country had caused all these problems in the hospital, and admired Muhammad and the other doctors and nurses for trying to save the lives of diseased and injured children.

Standing guard for twenty-four hours straight probably killed more brain cells than alcohol. It was mind-numbing. I smoked cigarettes, chewed Copenhagen dip, knocked back shots of Tabasco sauce, bought Coca-Cola from street vendors, wondered how Brandi and our boys were doing on the base in Colorado and whether the arm Adam had broken just before I flew to Iraq had healed, and I welcomed any distractions to stay awake. One distraction that I learned to anticipate and enjoy came in the form of daily visits from a young Iraqi girl who lived with her family in a house across the street.

I wish I knew the girl's name, but she spoke almost no English and I knew no Arabic. She was about seven years old. She had dark eyes, shoulder-length brown hair and—even for a young child—seemed impossibly skinny. She usually wore her school uniform: a white shirt with a blue skirt and a pair of sandals.

Every time I was stationed outside the hospital, the girl would run up to the fence that ran between us and call out the only English words she knew: 'Mister. Food.' Over and over she would say that, and I can still recall her high-pitched, breathless enthusiasm. She seemed fearless, full of energy, and not the least bit frightened by my M-249 machine gun. She acted as if she didn't even know that she lived in a war zone, and ran to the fence the same way my own children might have approached a sandbox, piping out, 'Mister. Food.'

During my first tour of duty in Ramadi in May, and my second time there in late June and July, I stood guard at that hospital on at least thirty occasions. She ran up to the fence every single time I was posted on duty there. I sat just inches away, on a big rock, but I would stand to greet her when she came. I wondered who had taught her to say two English words. Perhaps it was her mother, who often stood at the door of their ramshackle house, waiting for the girl to return with food for the family.

The first time she ran up to me, I tried to ignore her. We were under orders not to not to speak to Iraqi civilians unless authorised to do so by one of our officers. I knew that it would be better for me to have nothing to do with her, and it didn't seem like a good thing for a seven-year-old child to be anywhere near American soldiers standing with assault rifles locked and ready at all times.

'Mister! Food!'

'Go away,' I said.

'Mister. Food.'

I waved my hand to tell her to go away, because she clearly wasn't getting my words.

She kept at me, and I started mumbling at her. 'Come on, little sister, you've really got to get out of here.'

She stood motionless, kept smiling and would not leave. Finally, I reached over the four-foot high, chain-linked fence and handed her my MRE. It was a Beef Enchilada, with Tabasco sauce, a packet of cheese, a few crackers, two pieces of gum, a bag of Skittles, a pouch of powder to make orange drink, and a pack of matches. The whole thing came in a thick, tightly sealed plastic bag, about a foot long, six inches deep and three inches wide. It weighed less than a pound.

She took it, turned, and ran with it back to her house. I don't know how her family got into that thing. The instructions in small print on the bag were only in English. I don't know if her family members figured out that you had to break open one pouch, pour in water and let it boil for a minute or so before you ate it. I had no idea what a poor Iraqi family would make of food that was made to feed men on the moon. Perhaps it would be so bad that she would never come back.

But three days later, when I returned for another day of guard duty at the hospital, there she was, racing out of her house, across the small street and up to the fence where I stood.

'Mister! Food.'

Her face and her feet were dirty. It occurred to me that it must be extremely hard in Iraq to keep a child clean, in a country with a destroyed infrastructure and a ruptured water supply.

Once more I tried to wave her off, but she would have

none of it. She stood her ground until I tossed her an MRE. This time I had a different flavour stashed in my pants' cargo pocket: Country Captain Chicken, along with a package of peanut butter, a container of grape jam, a slice of bread in vacuum-sealed plastic, a piece of poppyseed lemon cake, peppermint gum, and the drink powder. I handed it over. She smiled, took it and ran off. But when she got to her front door, I saw her mother slap her and send her right back out to me.

'Mister. More food.'

A-hah. A third word.

She resisted my warnings to get clear of danger, and stayed until I managed to fetch another MRE. I radioed one of my buddies in the squad to get her another MRE from the APC and bring it to me. This time it was Beef Teriyaki.

She did not get slapped again when she returned with the second package, and I wondered if her family had ever seen peanut butter and jam, or what they thought of Country Captain Chicken. It struck me that they had a pretty dismal picture of American life: M-249s and the world's fastest yet least edible food.

As my guarding duties at the hospital continued, I began to carry a small stash of MREs so that I could give her two at a time.

The girl always ran home with them. She never walked. It seemed like running was the only speed she knew. It didn't matter if it was 125 degrees in the afternoon sun. When the girl moved, she ran. It made me happy to see her flying on those light brown legs across the street.

I wondered what sort of life she would have when the war ended. Would she continue in school? Would she end up becoming a doctor or a teacher?

Her visits were the best part of my days at the hospital, and she was the only person in Iraq—soldier, civilian or fellow soldier—whose smile I enjoyed. From my earliest childhood, I have distrusted the smiles of adults because I always wonder what they know that I don't.

The smile of this child in Ramadi brought me to thoughts of my own wife and children. I wished that Brandi could see this girl, and discover what I was coming to know: it was not true that all Muslims were terrorists, children included. The truth was that this little girl was the same as any child growing up in Guthrie, Oklahoma, Fort Carson, Colorado, or any other part of the world. All she needed was a little food, a little schooling, a clean supply of water and some loving adults to take care of her.

She was no terrorist. She was nothing but a child, and everything about her—waving arms, uncombed hair and torn sandals—was a reminder that she and her family had the same needs as me. All they wanted was food, water, shelter, safety, school and work—and who didn't?

I wasn't the only soldier in our squad who gave rations to the girl. Sykora did it too, and we spoke of her often.

'I saw that girl today, while I was out front of the hospital,' Sykora would say.

'Give her anything this time?' I asked.

'Damn right,' he would say. 'Beef stew and a bottle of water.'

I noticed little things about her as the visits continued. She seemed to have a slight limp when she ran. Each time she came, as soon as I tossed her one or two MREs, I would say, 'Hey there, little sister. You really have to get going. Go. Don't stay here. Go home now.'

I didn't want her to stay long, because every time Lieutenant Joyce saw me handing her food, he scolded me for fraternising with the enemy. When she stood too long at the fence, I would toss candies—Werthers and Strawbursts—far away to get her to move to a safer spot.

As for the MREs, I gave her a bit of everything we had, including Chicken Salsa and Beef Steak. It all tasted like dog food, but it could keep you alive in a pinch, and this little girl and her family needed them more than I did. When she got the food, she would smile, give me a little bow, turn and run back home.

After I had returned from Fallujah, the girl recognised me, perched on a rock at the corner of the fence, and began running to me daily again, asking for food. I would give her bottles of water, too.

One day, she brought me a piece of bread. When she passed it over the fence, from her hand to mine, I could feel that it was still warm.

'Fresh baked?' I said.

She smiled and waited for me to eat it.

It was a flat bread, and delicious, and she would not move

until I had eaten the whole thing.

'Thank you,' I said.

The next day she brought me a glass of water.

I knew it was probably straight out of the Euphrates River but I wanted to please her so I drank it straight away. It was nastier than hell, but I was happy to do that for her.

I was away on house raids for a few days after that, and I found myself looking forward to guard duty, so that I could see the little girl again.

The next week, I was back at my post in front of the hospital.

I saw the girl run out of her house, across the street and towards the fence that stood between us. I reached for an MRE, looked up to see her about ten feet away, heard the distinctive sound of American machine-gun fire, and saw her head blow up like a mushroom.

Her death was so immediate and such a shock that I couldn't believe what I had seen. I immediately looked around. There were no armed Iraqis in sight, and I had not heard any of the steady drilling sound made by the Iraqi AK-47s. The only thing I had heard was an M-16, which doesn't give off a loud, sustained burst of gunfire. It sounds much weaker than the AK-47, and shoots just a few bullets at a time. *Pop pop pop.* Break. *Pop pop pop.* Break.

I looked in every direction. The only armed people in the area were my squad mates, posted at various points around and on top of the hospital. My own people were the only ones with guns in the area, and it was the sound of my own people's guns that I had heard blazing before the little sister was stopped in her tracks.

I saw her mother fly out the door and across the street. I know that she and someone else in the family bent over the body. I could feel them all staring at me, and I could say nothing to them and do nothing other than hang my head in shame while her family took away the body.

Even today I can't help thinking that it was one of my own guys who did it. And I can't help feeling that I was responsible for her death.

If I hadn't been feeding her, and allowing her to believe that it was safe to come by daily to say 'Mister. Food' and to scoop up the MREs that I had gave her, little sister might be alive today. She would be ten or so years old now, around the same age as my eldest son Zackary.

Her death haunts me to this day, but I am trying to learn to live with it.

# SIX

# AL-HABBANIYAH

Near the beginning of August 2003, my Combat Engineer Company left Ramadi and moved about ten miles east to al-Habbaniyah. It was a small, dusty town of no more than 10,000 people, set on the banks of the Euphrates. Close to al-Habbaniyah, there was a village named Khaldia. In this book, when I write about events in al-Habbaniyah, I mean the area including it and Khaldia. We spent the next six weeks there raiding houses, patrolling streets, and guarding ammunitions depots and our own compound.

The Bible says that the Euphrates River was one of four

flowing out of Garden of Eden. I wish we had found peace by the calm waters bordering the town, but by this time tensions in Iraq had escalated so much that we were under regular attack from fighters we could never see.

As a group of soldiers, if we stopped in any one place longer than twenty minutes, mortars and rocket-propelled grenades would start raining in on us. When I found myself alive at the end of a dangerous day, I sometimes imagined that, just like a cat, I had been granted nine lives. Even so, they were being used up quickly.

Around this time, my squad mates and I were on foot patrol on the streets of al-Habbaniyah when rocket-propelled grenades started falling. I could hear them whizzing through the air. They were about half the size of football, but something of a blur as they flew by, just above my head. I would be injured if any of them blew up within thirty yards of me, and dead within ten yards.

I dashed for the cover of a concrete wall. Before I could make it, a grenade hit the ground just inches away. I expected to be shredded by red-hot shrapnel, but the grenade bounced, rolled and failed to explode. I kept running and took shelter behind the wall.

There was no wake-up call more brutal than a close encounter with a grenade. It was nastier than ten shots of Tabasco or five cups of coffee. As my pounding heart slowed I thought that sooner or later my time would come.

Being attacked so often by invisible enemies made all of the squad more and more anxious. We didn't like being shot at, didn't like having nobody to shoot back at, and we wondered if we would ever get home alive.

I didn't get to call Brandi often. About five weeks went by in Iraq before I could make my first call home, and usually three weeks would pass before I would have another chance. Sometimes I would stand in line for hours, waiting for my turn on a military telephone. Some days, I would get my two minutes on the line, and get through to my wife. Other times, before I could make it to the front of the line, I would have to report back to duty. I loved hearing from Brandi, and reassuring her that I was just fine, and I loved hearing her voice and receiving her weekly letters. Throughout my time in Iraq, however, the words Sergeant Jones had said, the day before I flew out from Colorado Springs kept ringing in my ears: 'Your wife is gonna start fucking some other guy the moment you're out of the country,' he had said. 'You wait. You'll see. It happens to them all.' That little bastard had known exactly how to upset me, and the seed of distrust embedded itself in my skin. In my mind, I trusted Brandi and believed that she would stick by me until death parted us. But my heart was a different thing, and my heart worried.

■

Some soldiers lost their lives in Iraq, and others lost their limbs, but I did know of a few who were worried sick about matters at home. One private from Alaska heard that his wife had developed brain cancer. After waiting some time, he was allowed to fly home.

Once, when I was next in line for the phone, I overheard a specialist in my company talking to his wife. There was no privacy whatsoever on the military telephones, and I could even hear her talking back to him. I could hear her saying that she was leaving him, and then I could hear a man bark into the line: 'Your little bitch wife is my princess now.' And then the line went dead.

I signalled to the fellow that I could wait and that it was all right with me if he called home again. He dialled the number and got his wife back on the line. She told him that he would be getting separation papers in the mail. The soldier broke down and cried just as freely as a child. There was nothing for me to do but put my arm around him and hold him as his body shook.

One soldier named Foster, from Indiana, was thrilled when he got the chance to go home on a short vacation. I wished him the best, but I wasn't optimistic about how things would go because we all knew that he hadn't received a single letter from his wife during our months in Iraq and his home telephone number had been disconnected. Foster was given two weeks off, but after ten days he was back. I asked him why he had returned early.

'My wife left me, sold everything we had, ran up our credit card and took off,' he said. 'I have nothing left, so I might as well be here.'

Our morale was dropping, but so was that of Sayeed, the nineteen-year-old Iraqi who travelled with our company. Since our first days in Iraq, he had been insisting, to me and some of the other soldiers, that our commanders had promised him that if he kept serving them for $20 a week, running errands and translating to and from Arabic, they would bring him to America and let him live there.

'It's a pack of lies,' I told him, 'and there's no way in hell they're going to take you back with them.'

'The captain said it was true, he knows more than you,' Sayeed said.

But as time went on, Sayeed saw no indications that he would be going to the United States. True, he kept drawing his $20 a week. But he also began getting death threats from Iraqis who saw him as a traitor. As the war in the country worsened, Sayeed became nervous and agitated. When he had first begun working for the 43rd CEC as an interpreter and errand boy, he had walked freely in the streets of Ramadi. But by the time we had set up in al-Habbaniyah, he would not leave the military compound without us. I wondered if he thought threats were worth his meagre salary and the shaky promise of a new life in America.

◼

Sometimes I hand-washed my underwear and socks and let them dry under the boiling sun, but I never had the chance to wash my sleeping bag. I spread it out in our new lodgings in al-Habbaniyah—as usual, a former military compound that had been blasted with our own bombs. We set up a gate around the compound, a dormitory and meeting quarters.

At night, all the soldiers in my platoon bunked together

in one room. We each had a cot, but they were only a foot apart, and it seemed that some of the men had given up entirely on sleep. Lying still on a cot could open the doors to memories and nightmares, and for some, it was easier to escape the night by watching movies on portable screens, playing GameBoys, reading books or masturbating. I had just as many anxieties as my buddies in Iraq, but was lucky not to have any sleeping problems. I could sleep inside a tank and through a mortar attack, so the sound of ten men snoring was nothing.

Each American military company was responsible for dealing with the bodies of civilians it had killed, so one of my first and most unpleasant duties in al-Habbaniyah was to build a shack to store dead Iraqis until someone came to claim them. We put the shack near our front gate, so relatives could retrieve their loved ones without entering our compound.

I began to discover that I was becoming almost as much a danger to myself as the Iraqi resistance fighters. Every time I stepped out of our compound gate, I was aware that I might not make it back alive. I frequently thought about shooting myself in the foot, so that I could be removed from war and taken back home. Other soldiers talked about doing it too.

With all the bullets and grenades in the air, we didn't think it would be such a big deal to take our own little shot. We didn't think of the pain, or the fact that we would be dealing with that injury for the rest of our lives. All we thought was that a well-placed self-injury was manageable, and that it would get us out of harm's way.

Back home in America, you would have to be pretty far gone to think seriously about shooting yourself. But in Iraq, with shrapnel exploding every day and notices being read to us almost nightly about our fellow soldiers killed in various parts of the country, and coasting on so little shut-eye that I felt like I was sleep-walking in my daytime manoeuvres, self-injury seemed like a normal thought.

We knew one man who had already done it and another who had spoken openly of suicide. Shortly before coming to al-Habbaniyah, a specialist named Love loaded his M-16 grenade launcher while he was standing on guard duty at our compound. I was changing the oil on our APC at the time, and was only about fifty yards away when I heard the thump of the grenade and the soldier screaming. Sergeant Fadinetz, a few other soldiers and I ran over to Love.

'What happened?' we asked him, but he would not say.

We could see that Love had shot himself in the ankle, and we called for help. After he was taken away for medical care, we never saw him again. 'Guess he's going home now,' I said. Wherever home was, we assumed that Love eventually made it there. It was a good thing the grenade had not exploded; he could have been killed.

I talked about the incident with buddies in my squad, but none of us judged him, because we admitted we had all thought about doing the same thing.

Another time, I heard about a sergeant in my company

who raised his 9-millimetre, semi-automatic pistol, banged himself on the head with it and said that he was going to kill himself. He too was sent home.

One day, Captain Bower walked into our sleeping area, told us to gather around our cots, and read us a notice passed down from his superiors. It said that any soldier who shot himself would be patched up in Germany and sent right back into action.

I believed he was serious and stopped thinking so much of hurting myself. Instead I often considered another strategy, and even tried it a few times. While we took cover from flying bullets and shrapnel, I sometimes stuck out my arm, hoping that an enemy bullet might smash into it. Luckily I wasn't very good at getting shot, and no bullet or scrap of red-hot metal took me down during the months that I served in Iraq. Others in my squad talked about doing this too, and we would sometimes joke about it after a fire fight.

'I guess you didn't manage to take one in the arm, that time,' I would say to one of my buddies.

'No, maybe next time,' the answer would come back.

Nevertheless, we resented the fact that we wore flak jackets of inferior quality, dating back to the Vietnam War. We may have thought about injuring ourselves, but that didn't mean we wanted to die.

One day in al-Habbaniyah, a colonel came to give us a pep talk. Just before we assembled to hear him speak, Captain Bower warned us to keep our mouths shut. After the talk, the colonel invited questions. Nobody said a thing. The colonel reassured us that it was okay to tell him whatever was on our minds. Specialist Williams, who was in the second squad of my platoon, asked why the men had not received proper flak jackets. I saw Lieutenant Joyce and Sergeant Padilla giving Williams the evil eye, and the colonel brushed him off.

A little later, Williams came up to speak to me. He was furious. 'They're docking half of my pay for three months, just for asking a fucking question!'

I estimate that he lost at least $2000 in salary, but we received the better-quality bulletproof vests—called interceptors—within a matter of days. A number of soldiers thanked Williams for speaking up, but nothing we said could bring back his docked pay.

Most of us in the platoon had one reason or another for resenting our superiors. One sergeant was disciplined because he was caught drinking liquor with us while on guard duty. He was the only one punished, because he was highest ranking, and that didn't sit well with him at all.

Like the other buddies, I nursed my own grievances. Chief among them was the duty that fell on my shoulders every second day: to ignite, stir and burn all the shit in our toilets. Perhaps it helped us all to have some trivial point to be angry about. Perhaps the anger motivated us to keep stumbling from one day to the next.

One day, however, something new replaced shit-burning as my pet peeve. I was sitting on my cot when one of Captain Bower's aides came for me.

'The captain wants to see you,' he said.

When I walked into the captain's makeshift office, he told me that Brandi had caused a disturbance on the base at Fort Carson. I had no idea what he was talking about.

'You'd better learn to control your wife, Private,' he said.

It crossed my mind that I stirred his shit too. I should have kept my stupid mouth shut, but instead, I said, 'That's kind of hard, Captain, when she's thousands of miles away.'

'Well, Private, because of that, you won't be getting any more rank,' he replied.

By that, he meant that I would remain a private forever, and not even reach the rank of specialist. It also meant my pay wouldn't increase.

I walked out of his office with one more thing to stew about and, perhaps, one more distraction from falling mortars and grenades.

■

Busting into and ransacking homes remained one of my most common duties in Iraq. I had done it in Fallujah and both times in Ramadi and now I found the tasks continuing in al-Habbaniyah. Before my time was done in Iraq, I took part in about 200 raids. But by the time I had made it to al-Habbaniyah, I had lost all belief that we had good reason for the raids. We never found weapons or indications of terrorism. I never found anything that seemed to justify the terror that we inflicted every time we blasted through the front door of a civilian home, broke every-thing in sight, punched and zipcuffed the men and sent them away.

I had no choice but to continue with the raids, and I remained the one who set the plastic explosive on the house, blew up the door and was the third squad member to run inside with my rifle locked and ready. But I had stopped shouting at people by the time I got to al-Habbaniyah, stopped roughing them up, and stopped stealing from them. I had no more heart for the work, and believed that it did nothing but intimidate the Iraqis, destroy their few belongings and make them to hate us.

We took part in many raids in al-Habbaniyah, but two stand out.

For the first, at 3 am we were told to get up and go to a home that was suspected of having a cache of weapons. They dropped our entire platoon of twenty guys off near the river, saying that the house was only 200 yards away. We couldn't find the house and got lost.

For a good hour we struggled in a rice paddy by the river. It was hotter than hell, even before dawn. Along with our regular equipment, we lugged pickaxes that we had recently received to use in our searches. Finally we came upon a house. It resembled the photos we'd been given. We punched our location into the GPS, and it matched the co-ordinates we'd been given.

It was a handsome two-storey house, and quite isolated. Along with my usual squad members (with the exception that Specialist Mason had returned home and been replaced by

Specialist Barrigan), I ran up to the house. As usual, I put the charge of C-4 explosives on the door and we blew it in.

As we charged into the house, women were staggering out of their rooms. Three teenage girls screamed when they saw us. Some of my squad mates grabbed them and held them at gunpoint, and the rest of us ran through the house. We found no men at all—just six more women in their twenties and thirties.

The guys in my squad couldn't find a thing—not even any guns—and it seemed that the more incapable they were of locating contraband, the more destructive they became. They smashed dressers, ripped mattresses, broke cabinets and threw shelves to the floor.

'What the hell are you guys doing?' I said. 'There's not even a single male in this house.'

But on they went, until somebody had the bright idea that weapons were likely to be hidden under the floor. Out came the pickaxes, and the guys started busting up the floor, going through the rug, the tiles, and into the concrete.

It was so ludicrous that it was almost funny. Here were my guys trying to break through a concrete floor with pickaxes. If weapons had been stored under the rug, you'd think that the tiles would quickly give way to a secret hiding spot—not a uniform foundation of concrete running across the floor. Ten or fifteen minutes later, when it became obvious even to the guys busting the concrete floor that there was nothing in the house but angry women, we went back outside.

I found Private First Class Hayes with a woman under an

empty carport. He pointed his M-16 at her head, but she would not stop screaming.

'What are you doing this for?' she said.

Hayes told her to shut up.

'We've done nothing to you,' she went on.

Hayes was starting to lose it, and we weren't even supposed to be talking to this woman. I told her that we were there on orders and that we couldn't speak to her, but on and on and on she bawled at Hayes and me.

'You Americans are disgusting! Who do you think you are, to do this to us?'

Hayes slammed her in the face with the stock of his M-16. She fell face down into the dirt, bleeding and silent. The woman lay still on the ground.

I pushed Hayes away. 'What are you doing, man?' I said to him. 'You've a wife and two kids! Don't be hitting her like that.'

He looked at me with eyes full of hatred, as if he was ready to kill me for saying what I did, but he didn't touch her again.

Then something happened that haunts my dreams to this day.

All the women were led back inside the house, and our entire platoon was ordered to stand guard outside. Four US military men who outranked us went inside with the women. They closed the doors. We couldn't see anything through the windows.

I don't know who the military men were, or what unit they

were from, but I can only conclude that they outranked us and were at least at the level of a first lieutenant or above. That's because our own Second Lieutenant Joyce was there, and his presence did not deter them. He was the highest-ranking soldier from the 43rd CEC at the house, and he would have had every right to question any person of his rank or lower who assumed control over our raid.

Normally when we conducted a raid we were in and out in thirty minutes or less. You never wanted to stay in one place for too long, for fear of exposing yourself to mortar attacks. But our platoon was made to stand guard outside that house for about an hour. The women started shouting and screaming. The men stayed in there with them, behind closed doors. It went on and on and on.

Finally, the men came out and told us to get the hell out of there.

It struck me then that we, the American soldiers, were the terrorists.

We were terrorising Iraqis. Intimidating them. Beating them. Destroying their homes. Probably raping them. The ones we didn't kill had all the reasons in the world to become terrorists. Given what we were doing to them, who could blame them for wanting to kill us, and *all* Americans? This sick realisation lodged like cancer in my gut. It grew, and festered, and troubled me more with every passing day. We, the Americans, had become the terrorists in Iraq.

A few days later, I used up yet another of my nine lives. Our platoon of three squads had been assigned to guard a public building used by local Iraqi officials. While we stood on guard duty, several rocket-propelled grenades came raining in on us. Three or four bounced off the hatch of my APC. I was standing just a few feet away, but miraculously, the grenades failed yet again to explode. We did what we always did in such circumstances—we blasted away with our machine guns at where we imagined our enemies were hiding. We didn't stop to ask ourselves if any civilians were in the area; on orders from our commanders we just lit up the area with machine-gun fire. As always, we had no real idea where our true enemies were, or if we hit anybody with our return fire.

A few moments later, we received orders to move out of the area, so we got on our three APCs and began travelling slowly back to our compound.

After about half a block, as our three vehicles inched forward in formation, with mine at the back, we saw Iraqis assembling. I assumed that because our machine guns had lit up al-Habbaniyah, people were coming to see what happened.

Among the onlookers was an older-looking man—perhaps in his forties or fifties—sitting in a chair near the side of the road. He wore the traditional white gown, and he was not armed. As we approached, he raised his leg to bare the sole of his foot at us, as a sign of disrespect. We all knew that this was the Iraqi equivalent of the middle finger—a clear 'Fuck you'. As I watched, Sergeant Gurillo—perched atop an APC

just ten feet ahead of mine—put the man in the sights of his
M-16 semi-automatic rifle. The M-16 has a lever allowing it
to be used as a machine gun or for firing single shots, and
Gurillo—a short, stocky guy who was known to us all for
getting love letters from both his wife and his girlfriend—
must have switched the lever to single shot mode. Gurillo
tipped the barrel of his M-16 down ever so slightly, squeezed
the trigger and shot the man squarely in the foot.

The man tumbled off his chair and onto the ground, and
was immediately surrounded by a crowd that grew louder and
angrier by the moment.

My APC stopped rolling. So did the other two.

From his position in the first APC, Captain Bower radioed
Staff Sergeant Padilla, who was standing in front of me on
top of our vehicle.

'Who shot that man?' Bower asked.

Nobody said anything.

'Did any one of you see who shot that man?'

Again, no soldier answered. Sergeants Padilla and Fadinetz
had been with me on top of our APC, other soldiers were
with Gurillo on his, and yet more soldiers were on top of the
first APC, but not a single person answered the question. I
knew that I would get in more trouble for opening my mouth
than keeping it closed, so I did the same as every other man
in my platoon: I didn't say a word. As the lowest-ranking
soldier in the three vehicles, I had no right to break the chain
of command by speaking to Bower, and I knew better than to
raise the matter later.

I feared that the crowd would riot, and was relieved when our APCs began moving again and slowly rolled away.

■

Not long after Sergeant Gurillo shot the man who dared to raise his foot at us, Captain Bower summoned us into the compound. He told us that a terrorist named Al Jawiri was holed up in a house, and that we were going to smoke him out. He said our operation was called Task Force 26, and that it would involve elite soldiers from other military units. Rangers and marines would join this raid but, as usual, the members of my squad were to go in first. Given the dangers, however, instead of blasting apart the door with C-4 explosives, Captain Bower instructed us to break down the door with our APC.

At this point, in the midst of our briefing, I lost it. I spoke up.

'If you're using Task Force 26 with fancy military people,' I said, 'why do you need our squad? You say this is the house of a known terrorist, and you're sending us in first? Looks to me like you're sending us on a suicide mission.'

The officer ignored me. But that day, I just couldn't control my own mouth.

I looked at Captain Bower and at First Sergeant Meyer standing with him and said, 'If anything happens to any of us, there's a grenade waiting on you two!'

Sergeant Skillings, my squad leader at the time, tackled me. He took me outside. 'What the hell are you doing?' he said. 'Do you know what kind of trouble you can get into for speaking like that?'

'That's how I feel,' I said. 'It's a damn suicide mission.'

'The only reason you're getting away with your loud mouth' he replied, 'is that you know how to fix stuff and hook up our air conditioners.'

We moved out to get ready for the raid. I travelled with my squad mates in our APC, and sure enough, we used it to ram through the door. We drove several feet into an open room, pulled back outside, stopped the vehicle, jumped out and raced in with our weapons. Inside, we found two men on the floor: one sitting and one lying down. Something was wrong. The two men were immobile. They were alive, and awake, and they showed no sign of injury. The men appeared to be in their forties or fifties. Both wore white robes. One had a moustache. But they remained utterly silent. Although we had just smashed into their home with an armoured personnel carrier, they weren't getting off the floor or even turning their heads.

There was hardly any furniture in that house. There were no other people, and no weapons or suspicious items. My squad mates jumped on the men, zipcuffed them and started hollering at them to 'Get the fuck up!' and 'Get the fuck out the door!' The Iraqis didn't move. When my guys started kicking and punching them, they didn't even try to block the blows.

'No!' I shouted. 'Stop! There's something wrong here. Look at these men.'

But they continued with the beating while all the others

waited outside. As minutes passed, I kept hollering at my squad mates to stop and to leave the men alone. Finally a medic ran in, waved a hand in front of the Iraqis' faces, got no reaction then told us that the men were mentally handicapped. I gave my squad mates so much grief about this that they got sick and tired of my bitching and sent me outside to pull perimeter.

These two Iraqis had been beaten up because they were handicapped and couldn't understand what we wanted them to do. But even once we understood this, we showed no pity and took them away just like all the other men we found in home raids.

It would have been a lot better if we had just left. But while soldiers continued to ransack the house—in search of terrorists that they would not find—I stood outside with the many soldiers assembled to take part in the raid.

Iraqi civilians began walking towards us. They wanted to see the house that had been rammed by our APC.

Apache helicopters hovered in the air, and our APCs and tanks were lined up outside. With this additional military support we had more firepower than I had ever seen in one place in Iraq.

It was an eerie morning, in the early dawn. There was light in the sky, but the sun had not yet risen. I felt a cool breeze, and held my position guarding the corner of the house. I noticed a man burning piles of what appeared to be Iraqi dinars across the street.

'What's he doing?' I asked Sayeed, our interpreter.

'He's burning all his counterfeit money before you guys go over there and arrest him.'

But nobody else was paying attention to the counterfeiter with his burning bills. The crowd continued to grow as people pressed forward to see the house we had rammed.

Suddenly, from the other side of the house, a shot rang out. I heard shouting and could hear Sergeant Padilla speaking with Sykora.

'I thought she threw a grenade, and that's why I shot her,' Padilla said.

Over my walkie-talkie I heard Padilla say that he needed two other soldiers to push the crowd away from a body so that he and Sykora could inspect it.

I had to stay put, holding my position for another thirty minutes. Finally, as we were given authorisation to leave, I met with my squad mates near the APC, where there was a body on the ground.

The girl Padilla had shot was about ten. She wore a school uniform and had blood on her skirt. I was struck by how little blood there was on the girl. I assumed that the bullet had entered her stomach.

As she was being lifted into the body bag and zipped up inside it, Sykora said that he had found no sign of a grenade or weapon on the girl. Soldiers in my squad lifted the bag and set it down inside our APC. The rule was that if we killed somebody, we were responsible for policing the dead. That meant that we had to get them into a body bag and take them until a relative came to claim them.

I stood guard many times during my months in Iraq. I guarded our own compounds. I guarded the Green Zone in the two weeks I spent there. I guarded a bank and a hospital and the perimeter of all the houses we raided. But the worst kind of guarding I was called upon to do—in Ramadi, Fallujah, al-Habbaniyah and elsewhere—was to watch as relatives came to claim the bodies of the Iraqi dead.

After Sergeant Padilla killed the child who was said to hold a grenade, I guarded her body too. We stacked the bodies in the small shack at the front of our military compound.

There were many other bodies waiting to be taken—sometimes as many as ten or twenty at a time—and it appeared to me that most of them came back with other platoons in my company. My first platoon had been responsible for a number of deaths already, but we were almost saintly in comparison to the other platoons, who often came back with numerous victims in body bags. Some of them even kept count of their individual killings. I was glad that I never had to enter an Iraqi's house with them.

I mostly avoided them, but sometimes overheard conversations when we were eating in the chow hall. We didn't all eat together, but could hear each other talking as we moved in small groups, in and out of the area.

'I got my first one yesterday,' one guy would say.

'So what?' somebody else would reply. 'Today I got number five.'

A day or two after Sergeant Padilla shot the girl, I stood on guard duty at the front gate, just a few feet from the shack with the dead bodies, when a group of Iraqi civilians began walking towards me. I could see them from two blocks away, and as they drew near, there was old woman dressed in black staring at me, right through me. As she put one foot in front of the other, she did not take her eyes off me or release me from the hateful glare that seemed to be saying, 'You are a monster. How could you do this? How could you kill the one I love?'

All I can remember about her, apart from the dark eyes radiating accusation and hatred, was that she was not veiled, had discoloured sandals, and fearlessly drew closer.

She dealt with an officer and the interpreter at the shack, and wailed with her relatives as they carried the body away. I wondered if she had come for the body of the little girl that Sergeant Padilla had killed. All I knew was that somebody she had loved had fallen from our bullets, and I felt nothing but shame and guilt as they walked away, carrying their dead with all the dignity they could muster.

Tears came to my eyes that day, though it wouldn't be the last time tears would come to me in Iraq. Indeed, as the days went on and the Iraqis kept coming for their dead, little by little my spirit broke, and it allowed for the thing that many men cannot do—but I knew enough to shield my tears from the men in my company.

Specialist Sykora was a friend of mine, and one of the few in the platoon in whom I would confide my thoughts of the war. Although he had been in the army for years, he did not appear to believe in the war any more than me. He had his wild sides, though. He talked all the time about professional wrestling matches, and he had a thing about looking at dead bodies.

One day, as I was walking past the special shack, I heard thumping inside. I opened the door, peered inside, and saw Sykora holding up a body in a zippered black bag. He raised it and dropped it like one might slam a wrestler in the ring, then picked up another body and slammed it down too.

I was nauseated, and backed out of the shed immediately. I didn't like ratting on my squad mates, but it just didn't seem right to let Sykora keep going.

I sought out Sergeant Fadinetz.

'Sykora has gone nuts,' I said. 'He's inside the shack, wrestling with bodies and tossing them every which way.'

Sergeant Fadinetz looked away. 'He needs to let out his aggression,' he said quietly. 'Let him have his fun.'

I had done my fair share of talking with Sykora, but after that point I stepped back from the friendship. He was just too much for me. I didn't see how anybody who looked straight into the eyes of a grieving mother could entertain himself by wrestling with corpses.

■

There was a sergeant named Mike Meinen in the first platoon of my squad. He lived in Boise, Idaho, with his wife, when he wasn't at war. A month or so earlier, he had handed out cigars to celebrate the birth of his daughter. I believe it was his first daughter, and I remember him saying that he hadn't been able to get authorisation to fly home to see her. Meinen was a good fellow, and we would chat sometimes as we crossed paths on our way to and from the urinals at night.

In late August, while I was doing guard duty at the compound, Meinen and two others were patrolling the streets of al-Habbaniyah when they came under attack.

Skillings told us that a rocket-propelled grenade of a type that the U.S. had given to Iraq during its war against Iran shot straight through the steel hatch of Meinen's APC. The grenade is made to penetrate steel and then explode, and it did its job to a T, slicing through the APC like a knife through soft butter and then splitting into shrapnel. The hot metal exploded inside the APC, cutting through everything it found. We Americans have good weapons, and I was told that we had used this one to fight in Vietnam. Meinen and two other men named Wyatt and Castro were helpless against the exploding grenade. They escaped with their lives, but not their legs.

The APC somehow made it back to our compound, and we raced to help our buddies. A helicopter got there almost as fast as us. As the three men were being airlifted for emergency care, I picked up Sergeant Meinen's leg and placed it next to him on the stretcher.

'Now I get to see my daughter,' he said.

He and the others were whisked away. We heard later that

all three had survived and been fitted with prosthetic legs, but in the aftermath of the incident, gloom descended over the squad.

My squad mates and I were ordered to clean the blood out of Meinen's APC, but we refused to do so. He was our friend, and we felt that it would have been more appropriate for someone in another platoon—someone who didn't know him at all—to be assigned that task. For once, our squawking was heeded. Someone else *was* given the job, though squad mates and I did have to wipe the blood off the weapons. I cleaned Meinen's rifle. It too had been ripped apart by the grenade.

■

Some men in my company wanted to take revenge, and to go out and kill as many Iraqis as they could. My own anger was reserved for the President of the United States and the military commanders who had put us in this war in the first place.

I could see no justification for our role in Iraq, and could not think of a single positive thing that we had done in the country. My friends had had their legs blown off, and what was it for? If I was sent home in a body bag, would history see me as a hero or as an accomplice to evil-doers?

To my way of thinking, only a hugely positive result—such as preventing genocide or the proliferation of weapons of mass destruction—could justify all the sacrifices that Iraqis and Americans were paying in this war. But several months into my active service, I saw no such positive results and no signs of them either.

Not long after that, while guarding a weapons depot in al-Habbaniyah, I confided in Specialist Sykora and Private Lewis. 'If I get a chance to get away from here, I'm never coming back.'

'If you run, they'll be all over your ass,' Lewis said.

I gave it no more thought. Stuck in the middle of a war zone, it was too much to think about what I would do in America, or how life might work out for me.

A few days later, I asked Sergeant Jones about the point of the war.

'There is no point, it's just your job,' he said.

'But what's the justification for this war?'

'The justification is that you signed a contract and you're told to be here.'

'But when do I get to go home?' I said.

'Private,' he said, 'we can keep you here just as long as we want, and we ain't never got to send you home.'

Not long after, while my squad mates and I patrolled the streets in our own APC, we passed under a thick grove of palms.

'If you guys were fighting against me right now,' I said to Sergeant Fadinetz, 'you would all be dead at this very minute. I would have strung a mine up in those trees, and I would have been hiding right behind that big rock over there, and the instant you people rolled under these trees, I would have hit the switch. And you know what, Sergeant? Every one of you would be dead.'

To my surprise, the sergeant did not lecture me for speaking my mind.

Softly, he told me, 'I'd do the same thing if people invaded America.'

That got me thinking. How would I react if foreigners invaded the United States and did just a tenth of the things that we had done to the Iraqi people? I would be right up there with the rebels and insurgents, using every bit of my cleverness to blow up the occupiers. I would dig a hole in my hometown in Oklahoma and rig mines in the trees and set them to blow up when the enemy passed below. I would lob all the mortars and rocket-propelled grenades I could buy.

No doubt about it. If somebody blasted into my home and terrorised my family in the United States, I would be a force to be reckoned with. I would invent my own booby traps and come up with the most unexpected methods of mayhem. I would give the occupiers hell and keep at it until I was dead and gone, twice over.

# SEVEN

# AL-QA'IM

After leaving al-Habbaniyah, we spent the second half of September 2003 in a 'Green Zone'. Located in the desert, hours from Baghdad, it was a fortified, protected oasis where thousands of American soldiers were sent to rest and relax. Outside the guarded gates, there was nothing but sand for miles in every direction—nothing, that is, except for the hundreds of Iraqi vendors who lined up along the road. As we inched forward in a military traffic jam, the vendors walked among our vehicles, waving their arms and selling cigarettes, soda, ornamental knives, blankets and clothes. I figured that every one of them had been affected by the war. We had bombed their cities, raided their houses and most certainly killed at least some of their loved ones, but they knew that we had money. I didn't imagine that the vendors had any other way to make a living, and I watched as they swarmed our vehicles.

Sergeant Fadinetz and Specialist Sykora jumped off our APC to snatch up Persian rugs for a fraction of the price they would have fetched back home. Later, in a postal station inside the Green Zone, they would mail them to their wives. Private Lewis spent $30 on an Iraqi military uniform, complete with stripes and awards. I wondered who it had belonged to, and what had happened to the man who had once worn it. I'm not a big spender and never have been. I bought a caffeinated drink called Red Bat, as well as Mond and Mikado cigarettes. Most of the soldiers hated the cigarettes sold in Iraq, but I liked them just fine, and appreciated buying them for an eighth of the price of American cigarettes.

Endless rows of huge tents had been erected in the Green Zone, and we set up our cots in one of them.

I spent my time sleeping, smoking, drinking pop, weight-lifting and hanging out with my buddies Sykora, Lewis and Connor.

I'm not much of a reader, but I stretched out on my cot and read *Into Thin Air* by Jon Krakauer, about a disastrous climbing expedition on Mount Everest. Krakauer brought such a keen eye to the fatally mismanaged climbing adventure that I found myself wishing he could have seen everything I had been through in Iraq so other Americans and I could read his analysis.

I also spoke to Brandi every day, a luxury I hadn't had since arriving in Iraq. There were a hundred telephones in one big room in the Green Zone, and thousands of soldiers lined up daily to use them. It often took an hour or two to get to a phone. Even when I climbed off my cot to call Brandi in the middle of the night, I still had to wait more than half an hour for a telephone. She reassured me that all was okay at home. Philip was a healthy, growing baby who slept through the nights. Adam, who had broken his arm, no longer wore a cast. Zack did his best to help out around the home, and asked every day if I was still away in 'Sergeant World'.

Brandi finally told me about the incident that had prompted Captain Bower to promise that I would not be promoted in rank because I had failed to 'control my wife'. Brandi had argued with a soldier on guard outside the Fort Carson military base. When she complained that the soldier picked her car for a detailed inspection, he called her a bitch. She jumped out and threatened to take a swing at him. From that point, the argument escalated. Nobody was hurt, but it created a fuss on the base. Somebody reported it to my captain in Iraq, who disciplined me as a result. On the phone, Brandi said she was worried that I would be mad at her, but I just laughed. I loved my wife, and had no desire to try to control her from any distance. I had seen too many grenades and mortars to worry about a tussle at Fort Carson. And I didn't care about not being promoted from private to specialist. I didn't want to be in this war anyway.

∎

A few days after arriving in the Green Zone, I called home with great news. Sergeant Skillings had told me that because I was low-ranking and already had a family, I would be next in line for vacation. He didn't say when I would be flown back to the States, other than that it would happen eventually. Brandi was thrilled. The enthusiasm and affection in her voice helped me stay settled and relaxed during my rest time. Apart from guard duty, we had no work to do.

It was indeed something of a shock to move into quasi-civilian life in the Green Zone. Overnight, I felt like I was light years away from my daily life for the last five months. I had spent so little time sleeping, and so much time raiding, patrolling, guarding and worrying when the next bullet or bomb was heading my way, that I found myself oddly uncomfortable in the safety and comfort of the Green Zone.

I also found myself increasingly resentful, because most of the soldiers that I met from other companies told me that they had spent the bulk of their time right there in the Green Zone. I didn't even know who to be angry at: the soldiers themselves, for being able to eat and sleep well and call their loved ones every day; or my commanders, for putting the men in the 43rd Combat Engineer Company in constant danger for months. I was so tired and messed up after the months of hard duty that I didn't even know what I wanted.

Part of me longed to stay safe, sleep more, enjoy the decent sanitation and call home every day on the telephone. But the other part of me—the part that has never known how to sit down and goof off—chafed at feeling so inactive.

There were many American women in the Green Zone. Some were soldiers: others officers. Sergeant Skillings warned us that punishment would be swift if we were caught having sex with any of them. Nonetheless, one day while I was waiting my turn outside a portable toilet—which seemed like a luxury in comparison to what I had known thus far in Iraq—a private tapped me on the shoulder, smiled and asked if I would like to sneak off for a fast fuck.

While my buddies snickered a few yards away, she said that they had told her I was a father of three.

'I want to get pregnant,' she said. 'It's the only way they'll let me go home.'

I grinned but did not budge from my place in line. 'Thanks, but no thanks,' I said. 'You ought to try Specialist Barrigan for that. He'll be game.'

I pointed him out to her, and Barrigan thanked me the next morning.

'No problem,' I said.

The guys thought I was crazy for turning down the offer, but I told them I was a married man. 'I've already had my fun,' I told them, 'and I don't want any trouble now.'

A few days later, I was propositioned again. This time, a lieutenant asked for sex. I refused again, and suspected that she was trying to entrap me. Word among soldiers in the

Green Zone was that some officers tried to lure privates into sex, only to bust them for breaking the rules. There was no way I was falling for that. I didn't want anything getting in the way of my trip back home. I kept to myself, pumped weights every day, and kept lining up at the telephones so I could hear Brandi's voice. It was fabulous to be able to call home every day.

I coasted along, then found out that I wouldn't be going home anytime soon. After two weeks in the Green Zone, Sergeant Skillings told us all to pack up our things. We would be leaving the next day for a Red Zone—by which Skillings meant another dangerous assignment—on the Syrian border.

We all groaned. All the guys in my platoon had been hoping to be sent home for a break. We felt we had earned it, after four months of hard duty and countless mortar attacks.

'Nobody's going home yet,' Skillings said. 'They need us for a tour of duty on the border. It's rough up there.' He told us that Americans had been meeting a lot of resistance near Syria. It would fall to us to stop terrorists from slipping over the border and into Iraq.

We loaded our APCs onto fifteen flatbed trucks and spent two days crossing the desert. When you crawl at twenty miles an hour with all your hardware tied down on trucks, you feel a bit exposed—like a line of ants on a beach. Although our army helicopters occasionally swept by for protection, we didn't stop for a moment. When I had to pee, I did like the others and aimed off the side of the truck. When other needs arose, I just had to wait. A military convoy doesn't stop for bathroom breaks.

At night, I sat back on top of the APC, stretched out my legs and looked up at the stars. Nevre in my life had I seen constellations as bright as in the desert. Shooting stars made me think of falling mortars. Even looking at the most peaceful sight in the world, I could not get my mind off war.

I didn't know we were going to al-Qa'im, until I saw a sign in English. It was a large but poor and dilapidated town of 150,000 people, on the banks of the Euphrates. It seems that the waters of that 1700-mile river flowed everywhere I went in the country. Perhaps, I felt, the river was keeping an eye out for me. With all the dangers we faced, something must have helped keep me alive.

There had once been a uranium extraction plant in al-Qa'im, but my own army had bombed it to smithereens in 1991 during the Persian Gulf War. The main thing now, I was told, was keeping an eye on the border traffic and to shoot anybody who tried to slip into Iraq at night.

My entire 43rd Combat Engineer Company bunked in a warehouse by an old railroad station, a fifteen-minute drive east of town. The senior officers had their own rooms, but the rest of us—more than 100 soldiers—slept together in one big room. Apart from our two-week break in the Green Zone, it was the first and the only time in Iraq that my platoon mates and I slept in a building that had not already been destroyed by American bombs. It was loud, having so many men snoring all at once, but at least I didn't have to worry about the roof caving in.

After temperatures around 120 degrees in southern Iraq, the nights in al-Qa'im—perhaps 60 degrees or so—seemed bitterly cold. Gloves kept my fingers warm, and I kept a stocking cap on my head to keep off the chill and to ward off the sand. Storms blew in every few days, driving sand over me and all my possessions—even inside the warehouses. In the morning, I would shake the layers of sand off my clothes and clean all the grit from my weapon, even though it had stopped working long ago.

In town, when I stood up on guard towers, I could see tanks blazing, jets racing, houses burning and explosions in every direction. It looked like World War III out there.

Border duty took up most of our time in al-Qa'im, but we kept raiding houses as well. We took mortar fire and rocket-propelled grenades almost every day we worked at the border. They tended to fall on us in the late morning or early afternoon. As before, we could never see who was behind the attacks, but our men would shoot in what they hoped was the direction of the enemy.

We often responded to mortar fire by raiding a house—any house—that seemed even vaguely to be near the source of the attack. I was standing on a guard tower early one afternoon when a mortar attack erupted, followed by our own gunfire. When the battle ended, our commander ordered us all into our APCs, so we could respond by raiding a house. Our three squads left the border, each in our own vehicle, made a quick turn and came upon a middle-aged, grey-haired man walking by the side of the road. His hands were empty, and nothing hung from his shoulders but a plain white robe.

From the first APC, Staff Sergeant Padilla radioed to our third vehicle at the back. 'Stop and apprehend that man,' he called out to us. 'He's in the area of enemy fire, so he's got to be guilty.'

The men in my squad jumped out of our vehicle, grabbed the man, pulled him inside and zipcuffed him.

Specialist Barrigan, who was new to our unit, grabbed a billyclub and started whacking the man on the head. When the man fell to his knees, Barrigan continued to beat him on the ribs.

'I'll keep his mouth shut,' Barrigan said as he pounded away, but the man remained totally silent. He gave no indication that he could speak English.

I felt terrible for him, having to lie down and submit to that beating while soldiers kept their guns trained on him. When the man was dazed and motionless, Barrigan stopped.

We returned to the border, dragged the man out of the vehicle and brought him into an interrogation room.

He remained zipcuffed and silent. Bleeding from the back of the head, he sat on the floor. I felt sorry for the fellow, and saw no reason for us to detain him. After an hour or so, while I stood outside guarding the door, an English-speaking Iraqi who worked at the border came into the room and spoke with Staff Sergeant Padilla. When he addressed our victim in Arabic, the detainee spoke back angrily.

'Release this man,' our interpreter said.

'Why?' Sergeant Padilla said.

'He works here at the border. He just finished his shift. He was walking home when you grabbed him.'

Our men cut off the man's zipcuffs, opened the door and sent him walking back home for the second time that day. He received no explanation or apology.

■

A few days later, our young interpreter Sayeed left us just as quickly as he had joined our company months earlier. He came to say goodbye.

'Why are you leaving us?' I asked.

'Captain Bower told me that I can't go to America,' he said.

I shook my head; I wasn't going to repeat what I had been telling him all along. Sayeed said it wasn't worth staying any longer. Not for $20 a week. Not now that Iraqis were threatening him for serving the Americans. And not after learning that all the promises made to him had been built out of thin air.

He extended his hand, and I shook it warmly.

I thanked him for all the things he had brought us. I knew that a number of Iraqis had threatened to kill him for helping the American army, and I hoped that he managed to escape from Iraq before it was too late. I would never see him again, but I keep on hoping that he and his relatives are safe.

■

My days at the border were long, but they were straight-forward. When the daily mortars fell on us, I took cover in a concrete shelter. As an American soldier, I could run into any building or shelter within reach when the attacks came. Although the mortars and grenades were aimed at us, they often fell near the drivers and passengers lined up in cars and semi-trailer trucks, waiting to cross over into Syria. Sooner or later, I was sure, travellers at the border would die—not because we killed them directly, but because we drew fire in the very spot where they were trapped in their cars.

One of my jobs on the border was to inspect the cars and trucks leaving Iraq. People were only allowed to take five gallons of gas and five cartons of cigarettes into Syria. My chief job was to find their extra stashes and confiscate them. Sometimes, when nobody was looking, I let people go across even when they were over the limit. I suspected that they were in desperate need of the gas and saw no reason to deprive them of it.

Although my buddies and I worked as quickly as possible, there was nothing we could do when the Syrians decided to shut down their border. Sometimes, the Syrian border closed for hours, or even an entire day. This created a massive build-up of vehicles but the drivers and passengers could do nothing except wait for the Syrians to open their gates again.

When the border did shut down unexpectedly, I some-times passed the time smoking and chatting with men who climbed down from their trucks.

One man asked where I came from.

'Oklahoma,' I said.

'Where is that?' he said.

'In the south.'

'The south?' he repeated, still confused.

I was going to explain where it was located, but the man raised his finger. He had something more pressing to ask.

'Your President Bush,' he began. 'Is he a good man?'

I turned to look in all directions. No American soldier was watching, or within earshot.

'He is a terrible president,' I said. 'If it was up to me, I'd be with my wife and kids back home.'

The truck driver seemed shocked. I guess he never thought that an American soldier would criticise his own leader.

'How long are the Americans going to be here?' he asked.

'Probably forever,' I said.

'We've got nothing to eat, and no money to buy anything,' he said.

I didn't know what to say to the man, so all I could do was give him a cigarette. He looked at it and raised his eyebrows.

'Mikado?' he said. 'Don't you have American cigarettes?'

'Sorry,' I said. 'Can't afford 'em on soldier's pay.'

He shook my hand and returned to his truck. As I watched him close the door, it struck me that if he made it through the day and got across the border, he'd probably be back a week later to wait again in the very same place. The only way truck drivers could make a living was to keep carrying goods back and forth across the border, no matter how dangerous the task.

■

Not long after a mortar attack on the border, I saw a man open his truck door and stumble outside. He had a hand over a gaping wound in his stomach. I feared that the guts would spill out of him and asked one of our medics to help him.

'I don't touch Iraqi blood,' the medic said.

I ran to the man and gave him some of my bandages, but I have no way of knowing if he survived that accident, or if he managed to get the shrapnel removed.

During my six weeks of duty in al-Qa'im, I was sent four times after mortar attacks to check on truck drivers who had been caught in their vehicles. On two occasions, dead men fell out from behind the wheel when I opened the truck door. The other two times, I had to pull the dead drivers out myself and lay them out on the ground. True, the Iraqis were killing their own people with those mortars. Still, I felt responsible. We had drawn the fire, and innocent people had caught it. Each time I pulled a dead man from his truck, I wondered whom he had last hugged on his way out the door, and if his loved ones would ever find out what had happened to him.

One day, Sergeant Skillings received a care package from his wife. Inside was one of the most treasured gifts of all—a two-pound tin of ground coffee. Skillings let us all share in the proceeds.

Sergeant Fadinetz and I frequently stood guard together on a tower at the border. The coffee helped us get through the eight-hour, all-night shifts. Fadinetz and I lugged a miniature, one-burner gas camping stove to the top of the tower, along with a percolator, the coffee, powdered cream and packets of sugar. One night, while we stood sipping coffee, I heard a *zing zing zing* sound.

'What's that?' I asked.

'Dunno,' Fadinetz said. 'Good coffee, though.'

I heard it again. *Zing zing zing.*

'Sounds like mosquitoes,' I said.

I heard it again, looked behind me, and just a few feet away saw little explosions against the concrete wall.

'Get down,' I shouted.

Another bullet grazed Fadinetz's helmet. We dove to the floor.

Fadinetz and I both had functional weapons on the tower—another soldier had lent me his for the night—but when we radioed our commanders, we were told to hold our fire. That ticked me off. I thought of all the times our men had beaten, shot at and even killed Iraqi civilians. But now, in a fire fight with bullets whizzing around me, I had to crouch low and hold my fire. Perhaps it was just as well that I was made to stay out of the fire fight. The shooting went on for an hour, but we escaped without injury. I don't quite know how we managed to get through that night without serious injury or death, but it didn't hurt to have the coffee sent by the wife of Sergeant Skillings. We had good coffee, which was a rare treat in Iraq, but I had paid for it with yet another of my nine lives.

■

I worked at the border along with Iraqi officials and police officers. I checked the dates on passports, while the officials read the details. I was supposed to teach these Iraqis the finer arts of ripping apart a car to look for hidden weapons and other forbidden materials. To protect the infrastructure of Iraq, no one was allowed to take windows, lumber or building supplies out of the country. I became pretty good at ferreting out hiding spots—under boards in trunks, behind false walls, and even inside spare tyres and jacks—but all I found hidden were gasoline and cigarettes. I found no sign of weapons and arrested no terrorists. One friendly police officer invited me home to have a meal with his family. I had to refuse, but he would sometimes bring me bread, cooked slices of lamb, and fruit. Sometimes drivers at the border gave me dates, and I usually passed them along to the police officer.

We had clear instructions about what to do if we saw people trying to sneak into Iraq at night when the border was closed.

Nobody was allowed to cross at that time, and if I happened to see someone trying to do so, I was to shoot to kill.

One morning at about 1 am, while I stood on a guard tower at the border, I spotted a man sneaking into Iraq. He was about two hundred yards from the gates that opened during the day for traffic.

I didn't shoot at him myself; it would have been overkill to do so. The men in my platoon were stationed on other towers at the border, and they opened up with a barrage of fire. Some of them climbed onto a humvee, swung into place a mounted, belt-fed, anti-aircraft weapon consisting of two linked 50-calibre machine guns, and drilled hundreds of rounds at the trespasser. He somehow escaped the first blast of bullets, and turned to run back to Syria. Still the soldiers kept firing away, and, after a blast from a weapon that would normally have been used against aircraft, the man's head exploded.

We were sent out to find the body. All I saw was blood and guts. I turned away from the carnage. I had seen enough to last me for a lifetime.

In the photo on the cover of this book, I am crouched next to an Iraqi man. He wears the traditional white robe. His wrists have been zipcuffed, and a burlap sack covers his head. I am expelling smoke from a cigarette. This photo was taken in al-Qa'im, and I cannot say exactly what motivated me to pose for it. One of my squad mates took the photo. I don't think that any other soldiers posed with the prisoner, but most American soldiers did take photos when they had the opportunity.

I did not beat the man, touch him or threaten him. I never even saw his face. We picked him up from a little bungalow— serving as a miniature detention centre—located at the head-quarters of my Second Squadron of the 3rd Armored Cavalry Regiment. Two soldiers guarded the front door of the bun-galow, and another stood ready at the gate where the prisoner was given over to my squad.

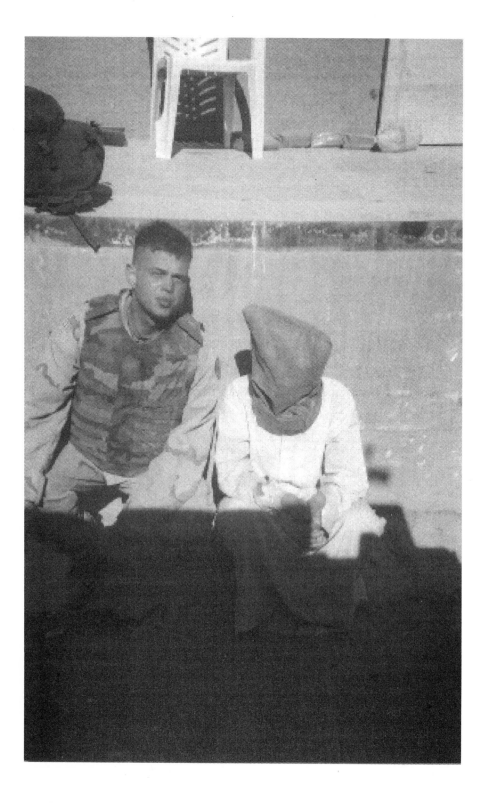

We were told to wait with him, just outside our APC, until we had authorisation to take him to yet another location. There, I imagined, he would be held until he was driven somewhere else yet again, eventually arriving at some sort of major detention centre. I had no idea who he was, where he had come from, why he had been detained or where he was being sent.

This was typical of the few experiences I had with detainees. Except for the ones I helped grab and zipcuff during house raids, I never saw where the men had been first taken or where they were going. And I rarely was in a position to witness how they were kept.

One morning when I was in Ramadi, while sitting on top of my APC outside a little house controlled by men from another platoon in my 3rd Armored Cavalry Regiment, I saw soldiers open the door and push a naked prisoner outside. The prisoner looked about forty.

One soldier kicked him as he stumbled out of the door and into the light, and another soldier kicked him as he passed through the gate. The detainee was sent to stand in the middle of the street, and for an instant I wondered why he had been brought out like that. And then, in full view of passersby, the naked man shat in the street.

I turned my head guiltily, but not before I had witnessed his humiliation. He stood up and was kicked on his way back inside the building. I never saw him again, and I don't know what happened to him. It would not be until much later, after I had deserted the army, that I heard of Abu Ghraib prison south of Baghdad, or about the abuses of Iraqi prisoners at the hands of Americans, or about human rights violations at Guantanamo Bay in Cuba.

While I was at war, I wondered where all the men that I helped arrest were taken, but at no time was I given any details, or taken to any of the centres where they were held in large numbers. The only thing I knew was that we arrested every male over five feet tall that we found in our house raids, and I never saw any of them again in the neighbourhoods that we patrolled day in and day out.

In al-Qa'im, the detainee who was taken out of the bungalow and given over to my squad wore nothing but white boxer shorts and a rough sack over his head. We received no explanation as to why he was unclothed. Our orders were to wait with him at our APC until given authorisation to drop him off with other soldiers. We gave him a white gown to put on, zipcuffed him and kept him for thirty minutes until we were told to drive him a few miles and drop him off with other soldiers.

He didn't say anything during the time that we held him. I don't even know he if spoke or understood English. Sergeant Fadinetz had a baseball bat at the ready, in case the man moved or attempted to resist, but he didn't use it, and I didn't see anybody lay a hand on the man or threaten him.

I regret posing for the photo. It was a stupid thing to do. Even at the time, I derived no pleasure from the man's misery. I would have offered him a smoke, if not for the bag on his head. As far as I was concerned, he was just one more Iraqi man who might never again see his family.

■

And now I come to the last story about my time in Iraq.

I was still in a Qa'im. I remained uninjured, despite all the bullets, mortars and grenades that had been shot in my direction. As far as I knew, I had not killed any person in Iraq. In fact, I had not fired my M-249 since it had stopped working a month or two earlier. I had taken part in about 200 house raids, but months earlier had lost any belief in the cause. Most of my buddies felt the same way. The house raids were nothing but an excuse to insult, intimidate and arrest the Iraqis. They gave us a convenient target to vent our frustrations at never having any real enemies to kill in battle.

For a time, the raids gave us an opportunity to beat people, steal their belongings and to destroy the things we didn't care to take. But I wasn't the only one who let up on the beatings and the stealing as my conscience returned. For most of us, setting off C-4 explosives, ransacking houses and zipcuffing teenagers and men provided a boost of adrenaline and excitement for a month or two at the most.

As time went on, we found no weapons of mass destruction. We found no signs of terrorism. We found nothing but people whose lives would deteriorate, or end, simply for having met us face to face in their cars and their homes. Some of us had not even respected them in death.

And so, while waiting to find out exactly when I would be allowed to return for a two-week vacation with my family, I found myself on duty as usual at the border in al-Qa'im. On this particular day, I was admitting people who were coming from Syria into Iraq, inspecting their passports and matching photos to faces. The travellers never had much more than the clothes on their backs, and we usually let them in without delay.

I found myself speaking with a young girl. I don't recall her name, or much about what she looked like, except that she was short, chubby and wore a black dress.

She spoke English well. She told me that she was thirteen, and that she was an Iraqi. She said she had been in Syria when war broke out with the United States, and was now returning to her family in Iraq. She was travelling alone, on foot, and had one suitcase. I checked the suitcase and found nothing but clothes.

I took her passport to an Iraqi official who was seated nearby in a shack. His job was to stamp the passports I brought him.

'What's this?' he asked.

'Just her passport,' I said, waiting for the stamp.

'There's no stamp showing when she left Iraq,' he said.

It didn't seem important, so I said nothing and waited for the stamp.

'How old is she?' he asked.

'Thirteen.'

'And she is travelling alone?'

'Yes.'

'Then she's a whore,' he said.

My mouth fell open. I stared in shock.

'What are you going to do with her?' I asked.

'Turn her over to the Iraqi police,' he said.

'Why don't you just let her go back to her family?'

'She's a whore,' he said again. 'I'll turn her over to the police, and we'll have fun tonight.' He rose from his desk to go look at the girl.

When we returned to her, nausea swirled in my belly. An Iraqi police officer stood by her side, smiling.

The border official told the girl that she was being turned over to the Iraqi police. Her eyes widened in terror. She didn't say a word, but I know exactly what her eyes pleaded as she looked at me: *I pray to God, please save me from these men.*

'Can't she just go back to Syria?' I said.

'Yes, Syria,' the girl said.

But the Iraqi police officer thrust his pelvis in a way that left no doubt about his intentions, gave the border official a big smile and left with the girl.

Before he'd left the area where my platoon was working, I hurried to speak to Sergeant Padilla and describe the situation. I explained that the cop had rocked his hips in anticipation of what he would do with the girl, and that he and the border official were working together.

'They're going to rape her,' I said. 'Isn't there anything we can do?'

'It's their problem, and none of our business,' Sergeant Padilla said.

I wanted to say more, but I also feared that my superiors would be happy for any excuse to punish me, and to deny me the opportunity to go home to my family. So I stayed silent, and I felt degraded by my own passivity and by that of my army.

By our sins of wilful neglect, we were about to have a child's blood on our hands. I knew it was wrong then, and now I know exactly what the Geneva Conventions say about protection of women and children in war.

> Women shall be the object of special respect and shall be protected in particular against rape, forced prostitution and any other form of indecent assault.

> Children shall be the object of special respect and shall be protected against any form of indecent assault.

I knew how things were going to begin for that thirteen-year-old Iraqi girl that day, but there was no telling how they would end. We had every means at our disposal to protect that girl. But we did nothing.

This is the last of my war stories. I dream of it still, and find myself waking and shouting out in the night. My own daughter, Anna, is not yet three years old. I can already imagine her questions one day, and I do not look forward to them.

■

A few days later, as we were nearing the middle of November, Sergeant Skillings told me to pack my bags.

'You're going home in two days. Two weeks off. Enjoy it.'

The buddies in my squad were happy for me, and they also knew that their turns for home leave were slowly inching forward.

Lewis asked me to bring him thermal underwear. Sergeant

Jones asked for a CD. Somebody gave me a letter to mail back home.

Sykora gave me a big hug. He said nothing but he told me, by the look in his eyes, that he knew I wasn't coming back.

The only person I dared speak to was Connor, the Texan with whom I had bullshitted about football and southern life during our whole time in Iraq. That night we sat on a flatbed railway car just outside our compound, while the other men were in their cots.

'This will be my last,' was all I said. I didn't say 'last day in Iraq'. I didn't have to.

'Well I'll be seeing you one day,' Connor said.

Sergeant Jones came up to me only hours before I left.

'You're coming back, aren't you?' he said.

'Yes,' I told him.

The truth was that although I didn't want to come back, I had no idea what I was going to do, or where my life would take me next. All I knew, for sure, was that I would soon be back in Brandi's arms.

# EIGHT

## AWOL

Six and a half months earlier, getting into Iraq had been a slow process. After a long wait in Kuwait, I had taken a slow-moving trip across the desert in a military convoy. But on the way out, they flew me by helicopter from al-Qa'im to the same Green Zone (al-Asad) I had stayed in during the second half of September. After a few hours, I was then flown by helicopter to Baghdad airport. There was nothing to do but wait, and that was a good thing because my mind was fried.

Apart from two weeks of rest, I hadn't slept more than an hour or two at a time for more than half a year at war. I had heard so many machine guns and mortars that I often found myself hard of hearing after fire fights. I could hardly string three clear thoughts together. I only knew two things for sure: my own army had made me ashamed to be an American, and I was finally going home to see my wife and children.

I didn't know what I would tell Brandi, but deep down, seeds of worry began to take root in my gut. If I told her that I was thinking about not returning to Iraq after the vacation, what would she say? Would she be furious? Would my lack of patriotism disgust her? Would she lose all respect for me? I wasn't sure if it was safe to tell her any of my worries, so on the long trip home I tried not to think about anything.

In the Baghdad airport, I ate an MRE, found a spot outside by an airplane hangar, rolled out my bag and went to sleep. My next flight was on a C-130 to Kuwait, with about one hundred soldiers. I knew none of them. I wore earplugs to drown out the noise of the engines and kept to myself.

Getting off the plane in Kuwait, we had to wait in line outside a security tent. Soldiers were not allowed to take weapons back home, and we were invited to leave guns and knives in an amnesty box before getting checked. I had dropped off my M-249 in al-Qa'im, and I had already turned in my M-16 at the Green Zone.

Twenty officers checked the bags of soldiers who were travelling back home, but there were so many of us to process that it took two hours to move through the line. I saw one inspector fish a grenade out of a soldier's suitcase. No big deal was made of it. When I was finally next in line to have my bags inspected, I watched a soldier up ahead to the left. An officer picked through his bag, and even patted down the clothing. The officer shook open an extra pair of army pants, rifled through a pocket and pulled out something thick.

'What the hell is this?' the officer said.

'An ear,' the soldier said.

'Soldier, you want to take a human ear back to the United States?'

The soldier, who made no reply, was removed from the line and taken away.

When my turn came, a woman began to inspect my bag. She had overheard the exchange, and smiled at me and shook her head.

'I guess some people want to take some pretty dumb-assed things home,' I said.

'You can't take all these cartons of cigarettes, soldier. Two is the max.'

'Okay,' I said, 'take 'em.'

When she saw that I didn't mind, she said in a low voice, 'You think that guy with the ear is bad. Last week, I caught someone trying to bring home a human arm.' She was laughing as she talked about how she had to pull him from the line and leave him with a more senior officer.

I didn't blame her for laughing. She must have seen her share of crazy stuff, and laughing probably helped her get through it.

'If he was trying to do that,' I said, 'he must have really

lost it a long time ago.'

She confiscated my cigarettes and let me go.

In the airport in Kuwait and on the long flight to Dublin, most of the soldiers wore cleaned and pressed uniforms. I, however, was not exactly dressed for Sunday church.

I wore the same dirty, bloodstained BDU (Battle Dress Uniform) that had kept me clothed for more than six months in Iraq. I had an extra, cleaner uniform in my travelling bag but I didn't want to put it on. I didn't want to dress up. I didn't want to look good. These were the clothes I had worn while at war, and I was disgusted by all the things I had been required to do. I didn't want to put a pretty face on things now, and I didn't care if my trousers and shirt hadn't been properly washed in months.

On the flight to Ireland, an officer gave me a righteous look. 'Soldier, didn't you have a better uniform to wear home?'

'No I didn't, Sir,' was all that I said.

I was tempted to tell the officer that I had been saving my second uniform for a special day. I had thought, throughout my time in Iraq, that I would put it on when something truly good happened. But nothing good did happen, so I never put on the second uniform. Eventually, wearing the same gear day in and day out—and washing nothing but my underwear and socks—became my own private fashion statement: given the things I had been made to do, why should I give a fuck about the way that I looked?

The officer stared at the bloodstains on my trousers, but I didn't want to meet any roadblocks on my long journey home, so I kept my mouth shut.

When we landed in Dublin, it struck me that I had not had an ounce of alcohol for months. A sergeant stepped out of the airplane, took a look at me and said, 'Soldier, let's go get drunk.'

We only had half an hour or so, but I slammed back eight beers as fast as I could. Nobody gave me a second look, because just about every American soldier in the airport bar was keeping pace with me.

It takes about seven hours to fly from Dublin to Atlanta. I took every free drink that they served on that flight, and tried not to think about which was worse: beating up and killing Iraqi civilians, or refusing to do it any more and becoming a criminal.

Getting off the plane in Atlanta, I found Vietnam War veterans lined up on the tarmac to clap and shake our hands and to greet us as war heroes. I didn't want to shake any man's hand. What had I done that merited a handshake? I got away from the veterans as quickly as possible, drank while waiting for the next flight, drank en route to Dallas, and sat in the first bar I could find in the Dallas airport.

There, I didn't have to pay for a single drink. First, a man wearing cowboy gear from head to toe called to the barman, pointed to me and said, 'I'm paying for everything this soldier drinks.'

He came to sit and talk with me, and said he owned a ranch.

'How's it going over there in Iraq?' he asked.

'Have you been watching news on TV?' I said.

'You bet,' he said.

'Well whatever they're showing, I can guaran-damn-tee you that it's not like that.'

'How so?' he said.

I told him that innocent civilians were dying and that I didn't think I wanted to go back to it.

He gave me his name and telephone number, and told me that if I ever went AWOL, I could come see him for a job on his ranch. I took his paper, but knew I would never call him. People say all sorts of things they don't really mean.

When the cowboy left, a woman took his place as the buyer of my drinks. When I headed to the bar to clear my bill, she called out: 'It's mine, I'm paying for it.'

When I walked to the gate to fly the final leg home, I was so drunk that I left my bag in the bar. They had to page me to go back and get it. I doubt they would have let me on the flight had it not been for my soldier's uniform.

■

Brandi didn't recognise me until I walked right up to her.

'Oh my goodness, you look like a skeleton,' she said. We threw our arms around each other. When we finally pulled back from the hug, she kept feeling my arms and my shoulders.

'Josh, there's nothing left on you,' she said.

'Army food,' I said, 'isn't quite as good as yours.'

'So does that mean you're going to start eating vegetables?'

'Give a soldier time to adjust,' I said.

Brandi did not take a step without keeping her hand in mine, or on my arm. 'I guess you had a few drinks on the way home,' she said with a smile.

'One or two,' I said.

She took my arm firmly as we walked into the parking lot. She is a good woman, my wife. She didn't say one bad word to me about arriving home as drunk as a skunk. She just took my hand and led me home.

Zackary and Adam, who were five and three, dove into my arms. Philip, who was just over one, didn't know who I was. No matter. I spent the rest of the day loving them all, and even Philip knew I was his father by the time he went to bed that night.

■

Back home in Fort Carson, my nightmares continued. I dreamt of decapitated heads, staring at me and calling out accusations. I dreamt of children dying. I dreamed of being in a fire fight with no bullets left in my M-249.

A day or two after I returned, I drank again and I blacked out. I don't remember what I did at the time, but Brandi told me that I had screamed out something about an attack and ripped the light fixtures out of the ceiling.

Every day of that two-week holiday, even stone sober, I kept reaching for a gun that wasn't on my shoulder. I felt naked without it. I couldn't stand in supermarket lines, because I was afraid that someone would throw a grenade or bring out a knife.

Brandi says that I was not the same man who had left just seven months earlier. I had no patience for crying children, couldn't walk outside without looking over my shoulder, couldn't get into bed without screaming in my sleep, couldn't stop mumbling about Iraq, and couldn't pay attention to a single household detail.

America felt like a dreamland. It seemed that not a soul in the country had the faintest clue about what I had been living every day in Iraq. My buddies were in danger, and I couldn't stop thinking about them. But outside the military base, people in Colorado Springs carried on as usual—going to work, sporting events, malls and movies. Walking about the city, a person visiting from another country would have had no idea that the United States was at war. The long, slow build-up to Christmas seemed to be the only thing that excited the people of Colorado.

But when I woke and when I went to bed, and when I ate and when I drank, I could not clear my mind of the places I had been: Ramadi, Fallujah, al-Habbaniyah and al-Qa'im. I imagined that the house raids and traffic checks continued, and that American soldiers were still bombing, shooting and beating Iraqi men, women and children in their homes, cars and streets.

I got drunk at a bar in Colorado Springs. Brandi says that I started shouting at her about how she and the children lived like royalty in comparison to the people of Iraq. Families over there had nothing to eat and nowhere to live, I hollered, and Brandi stared at me, wondering why I appeared to be blaming her.

'Just be thankful that our family doesn't have to live like that,' Brandi said, pulling me from the bar. Deep down, I worried just exactly how we would be living if I paid attention to the thoughts of escape swirling in my mind.

In the second week of my vacation, I settled down enough to move Brandi and the children off the military base at Fort Carson and into a private apartment in Colorado Springs. It wasn't part of any plan to go AWOL or to run from the military. It was simply that Brandi hated living on the base and being surrounded by army life.

We only spoke once or twice about the possibility of going AWOL. I didn't say much. I only said that innocent people were dying at the hands of American soldiers and that I didn't want to go back to the war.

'If I run from duty, we would have to go far away,' I said.

'Where would we go?' she said.

'I don't know,' I said.

Brandi didn't get angry, and she didn't try to tell me what to do. But neither of us had clear ideas about what we would do if I didn't return to Iraq. If I ran from duty, where would we live? How would we eat? How would we take care of our three boys?

All the time that I had been away, Brandi had been receiving my $1200 monthly cheque. But with rent, clothing, diapers and food bills, my salary had been barely enough to keep the family going. We had no savings in the bank and less than $200 in our pockets.

My conscience told me that it was wrong to return to Iraq and to keep doing things that I knew to be wrong. But the very thought of going AWOL overwhelmed us. It was clear that we could never go home to our families. They had no means to support us, or to protect us from army officers who would most surely be lying in wait. We had nowhere to run to and nobody to advise us, so we dropped the subject of my running from army duty before we had even discussed it seriously.

I spent the second half of the vacation unpacking boxes in our new apartment and sticking close to Brandi and the boys. They were the only people in the world that I wanted to see. I barely went out, and barely saw a soul. I made no contact with anyone at Fort Carson, and didn't even see or call the wives of the men in my company. I spoke with my mom and a few other relatives by phone, but didn't tell them anything about my problems. In fact, I was so overwhelmed by daytime anxieties and bad dreams at night that I did not even know that President George W. Bush came to speak at Fort Carson in the very days that I was huddled at home with my family.

Much later, when I learned of his visit, I went online to see what President Bush had said on 24 November 2003 to the troops at the Butts Army Air Field in Fort Carson.

> We're at war with terrorists who hate what we stand for: liberty, democracy, tolerance and the rights and dignity of every person. We're a peaceful nation, yet

we are prepared to confront any danger. We are fighting the terrorists in Iraq and Afghanistan and in other parts of the world so we do not have to fight them on the streets of our cities. And we will win. In this war, America depends on our people in uniform to protect our freedom and to keep our country safe.

I can imagine this speech being televised live to the troops in Iraq. I can imagine returning at four in the morning to Saddam Hussein's bombed-out palace in Ramadi after raiding and ransacking a house and detaining the males—even a fourteen-year-old boy who stood as tall as his father.

If my buddies and I had sat in our bloodstained Desert Camouflage Uniforms and watched a live broadcast of our president's speech, we would have thrown our rations at the TV screen. If our president stood for the rights and the dignity of every person, why had he sent the 3rd Armored Cavalry Regiment to war against Iraqi civilians?

I was required to check in with American army officials in the Dallas airport on 2 December 2003. My wife was even more upset to see me leave after the two-week vacation than she had been when I had left the first time. It would have been horrible to say goodbye under any circumstances. But it must have terrified her to see me like that—having lost a quarter of my weight and half of my mind—flying back to a war that I did not believe in.

Brandi cried at the airport, but I did my best to hold back the tears. I could not have other soldiers seeing me like that.

I got on the airplane and flew south to Dallas, but I did

not have one sip of beer. I was completely sober.

I looked out the window at 32,000 feet. I felt that I had been out of my mind to get on that airplane, and resolved to do something about it.

My stepfather, J. W., and my brother Tyler had arranged to drive from Oklahoma to see me off at Dallas. I met them when I got off the plane. Tyler gave me a big hug, and J. W. shook my hand as if I was a war hero. J. W. went on so much about how I was serving my country and stomping out terrorism that I had to tell him to shut up. I didn't tell him what I had seen in Iraq. I just told him to be quiet.

While J. W. waited in a lounge, Tyler stood with me while I checked in at the US Army counter.

'Your flight to Kuwait has been delayed two or three days,' an officer told me. He began to give me information about a hotel room the army had arranged, but in my mind the switch had finally clicked. I was not going back to Iraq.

'It's okay,' I said. 'I'll stay with my brother, in town.'

The officer gave me details about the new flight, but I didn't hear a thing he said. As Tyler and I walked away from the desk, I barely looked at the papers I had been given.

I called Brandi from the airport, and told her my flight had been delayed. We lamented about having been cheated of a few more days together. I promised to call her back that evening.

J. W., Tyler and I drove to a restaurant. I ordered a steak.

'How about a beer?' J. W. asked.

'Just a Coke,' I said.

J. W. raised his eyebrows. He could not drink any longer, because of his liver transplant, but to him it didn't seem right for an off-duty soldier to pass up a drink.

We didn't stay at the restaurant long. J. W. and Tyler wanted to hurry back to their hotel to catch an Oklahoma Sooners football game on TV. Funny. In Iraq, I had talked constantly with Connor about the Sooners, but now that I had returned from war I had completely lost my interest in football and other sports. Once I had been a sports fanatic, but they spoke to me no longer. It would have been nice to be able to knock back a beer and lose myself in a few hours of televised sport, but three other things teemed in my brain: I wanted to hold my wife and children; I had the blood of men, women and children on my hands; and I couldn't live with myself if I had to fight again in Iraq.

I called Brandi from the hotel room while Tyler and J. W. watched the Sooners play. My mind was made up, but I couldn't tell J. W. He might try to turn me in to the military police at the airport if he heard that I was planning to go AWOL. That night, after J. W. retired to his own room, I spoke privately to my brother.

'I'm not going back,' I said.

'What do you mean?' Tyler said.

'Just what I said. I'm not going back to Iraq.'

'What's going on over there?' he asked. Tyler was nineteen at the time. Back home in Guthrie he had a job with a land-scaping company.

'I don't want to talk about it,' I said. 'It's fucked up.

Innocent people are dying over there. It's not the war you think it is. I'm not going back.'

'Well, what are you going to do?'

'Go back to Brandi and the kids.'

'But what are you going to do when you get there?'

'I really don't know. But don't tell anybody, okay?'

'I'm your brother, Josh. I'm not going to say a word.'

At six in the morning, I persuaded J. W. to drive me to the airport and to pay for my one-way flight back to Colorado Springs.

'Do you have authorisation to go back home?' he said.

'Yes,' I lied.

'Do you know when you have to be back?' he said.

'Yes.'

I called home again from the airport and told my wife I was coming home. I didn't say why, but took comfort in the knowledge that she would be happy to see me in any event.

I caught the first flight to Colorado Springs, took Brandi into my arms again and told her I was not going back to Iraq. That day, I called the office of the Judge Advocate General—a sort of military lawyer who is paid to advise soldiers in distress.

I didn't identify myself. I just said that I was thinking about not returning to duty. He told me to think hard on the matter and to call him again the next day. When I called him back and explained that my conscience would not let me return to war, he became hostile. 'Soldier, you can do one of two things. You either get on that plane and get back to Iraq, or you go to jail.'

I hung up.

Brandi and I had to lie low until we could find some money. We put off paying every bill that came due—rent and everything else. We bought nothing but basic food for our family: bread, peanut butter, noodles, canned sauce and milk. I stayed away from Fort Carson, and knew it was a lucky stroke that we had moved off the base. The people there had no idea where I was, and I wasn't about to let them find me now. I stayed in our apartment as much as possible, to avoid being seen on the streets. It helped that my entire company was in Iraq, and that nobody on the base knew my face.

I stayed in hiding for close to two months in Colorado Springs. Before we could leave, though, I needed a bit of money. Early in January, I prepared my tax return, took it to an H&R Block office and got a refund of about $500. That was what I had saved in taxes, as a result of serving my country overseas. My mother sent us some money. Brandi had made a friend in Colorado Springs, and without her support and her money, I don't think we ever could have made our escape.

Our Ford Aerostar van was falling apart, so I sold it to a neighbour for $100 and bought a broken-down, twenty-five-year-old 1978 Camaro for $700 from the son of an air force colonel. I put a minimal down-payment on a rent-to-buy Compaq Presario laptop computer, took it with me and never made another payment. Both Brandi and I were inexperienced with computers, but if we were going on the run, I knew that I would need to be scouting for information on the internet. And using my military ID, I arranged to rent a U-haul for five days.

Finally, in early February 2004, Brandi, her friend, the children and I took off.

I drove the U-haul with Philip in a car seat, and the women took the Camaro with Zack and Adam. The Camaro ran, but that was about all I can say for it. It had holes in the floor-board and in the tailpipe. Exhaust spilled into the car, which forced them to drive with the windows down.

Our first stop was Louisville, Kentucky, but I felt nervous staying there because it was too close to the Fort Knox army base. So we didn't even spend the night in Kentucky state. We drove onto Trenton, New Jersey, but I was anxious and nervous and the city seemed too rundown for my liking. Still, rundown was exactly what we needed.

I had come to the conclusion that a city in the northern states was where we had to hide. It had to be a city where nobody knew us. It had to offer countless places to disappear. It had to be a city that was rife with crime. It had to be a city with plenty of people passing through, so that licence plates from Colorado wouldn't attract attention. It had to be a city with so many thefts and murders that police would have bigger things to worry about than a poor family in a broken-down Camaro.

We picked Philadelphia, and spent the first night in a highway rest stop out of town.

I found a storage facility for all the stuff in our rental truck and abandoned the U-haul in the parking lot of a suburban mall. Then, I got on friendly terms with a security guard who kept watch over the highway rest stop where we slept in our car. Until we could start making money, we couldn't afford to pay for any lodgings. I didn't tell him anything about my problems, except that we were a family that had fallen on hard times. It's lucky for me that from time to time, people have looked kindly on my family and me. The security guard was an older black man, and he seemed to accept—without the need for explanation—that we could use a little help. He said we could camp out at the rest stop during his night shift but that we would have to be gone by seven each morning.

Our friend found a job within two days as a waitress for a restaurant called The Dining Car. Brandi found a job just as quickly, also as a waitress, at the Olympia Café. It paid $2 an hour, plus tips. They pooled their slim earnings to keep us going.

I spent my time watching the kids and being paranoid. It was not easy to watch my kids at a highway rest stop, or to move from rest stop to mall and back to another rest stop while Brandi was working. Somehow, I made it through enough days until we had money to pay for a room in the cheapest, sleaziest hotel we could find. They gave us one room for $350 a week. All six of us slept in it together. We had to pay the money up front, but at least that kept me off the streets for a while.

While the women worked, I took care of the children in the hotel room. I made them stay quiet, and played games with them. For entertainment, I let them play in the back parking lot, while I sat close by on some steps. But even that was a risk, and before I let the children out, I peered out every window for signs of men with crew cuts, four-door sedans with Colorado plates, or military stickers on cars or licence plates. And I kept myself ready to run, in case I spotted somebody on my trail. At all times I had a knapsack within arm's reach, continuing a few clothes, a bit of food, some money and maps of the city. I memorised bus and subway routes. And I never left any room without peering through the curtains.

I felt paranoid each time someone looked at me in the street, and guilty about making fugitives out of my wife and my boys. The children spent most of their days locked inside hotel rooms, and I was sure that I had ruined their lives. Still, Brandi stuck with me. She never doubted me, never questioned my decision to run from military service, and never demanded detailed explanations.

About Iraq, I said very little except that innocent people were dying and that I would not take part in victimising civilians any more. That was enough for Brandi, who would take my hand when I spoke. 'If they're doing bad things, then you can't go back there,' was all she said about it. I'm not sure if she understood that by helping me run, she was doing far more than standing beside a fugitive husband. She was helping to keep me alive, and helping to keep me from mental collapse.

We changed hotels every month. A hotel needed certain qualities to be suitable for fugitives. It had to be cheap. It had to have staff who would take our money without asking for ID, who didn't care who stayed there, and wouldn't complain about six of us staying in one room. They had to be willing to overlook the fact that we hooked up a microwave and a toaster oven wherever we went.

Our breakfasts consisted of cold cereal and milk. I'm addicted to coffee, but we didn't even have that. Lunches and dinners were always the same: bread, sandwich meats, peanut butter, and potatoes that we bought in large economy bags. We baked the potatoes in the microwave, or sliced and toasted them in the tiny oven.

Most of the hotels offered internet hook-ups, and I started punching words like 'AWOL' and 'soldier needs help' into various search engines. For the longest time I found nothing at all. I saw details about the GI Hotline, but I couldn't imagine that any American organisation would be of help to me now. But I kept on believing that somebody, somewhere might be able to help us.

Not long after we arrived in Philadelphia, our friend told me that the owners of The Dining Car were looking for a dishwasher. I began working there at night, after Brandi had finished her restaurant shift. I changed my routes every time I drove to work. I looked constantly in the rear-view and side-view mirrors. Once or twice police officers followed my broken-down Camaro, but I had planned a strategy that worked in the short term: when I was being tailed, I drove into a wealthy neighbourhood, parked in the driveway of a pleasant house, got out of the car and walked to the door. I did my best to act like I belonged, and the cops seemed to buy it the few times that they followed me.

The dishwashing job paid about $7 an hour, and I kept it for about two months. We continued living by the skin of our teeth, and when money was too tight to pay for a hotel room one week in advance, we returned to the highway rest stop with the sympathetic security guard. We could camp out in our car from time to time, as long as we arrived after ten in the evening but left before seven in the morning. Rental apartments, no matter how cheap, were out of the question. We did not want to give our identification or our social security numbers to anyone.

It was lucky for me that no police ever pulled me over in the Camaro. The registration had expired, and so had my driver's licence. I had no automobile insurance. If anybody had punched my name into a police computer, I would have had handcuffs around my wrists in no time. Brandi, however, was pulled over twice, and once given a ticket for driving without an inspection sticker proving that the vehicle was roadworthy. Fortunately, I was not in the car on either occasion. When she told me about these encounters, it made me even more resolved to keep my head low in the city. Every night I watched the news to see if the American government had begun some sort of crackdown on war deserters.

After a few months in Philadelphia, a job advertisement in the paper led me to try my luck at the Curtis Elevator Cab Company. I asked if they still needed a worker and was told to return the next day. In June 2004, I began working for $12 an hour—more money than I had ever made in civilian life—making the insides of elevator cabs. Two brothers, Rich and Bob Andrews, ran the company, and seemed to be happy with my work. I made the insides of elevators: the panelling, the railings, the boxes that held the buttons and the light fixtures. I was employed as a general labourer and machinist, welding, using shearing machines and presses, and working with wood and glass.

I made myself as useful as possible. I wanted to keep the job and make money, and didn't want to have to look for another job until we knew what we were going to do in the long term. I had already decided to give them my real name and my real social security number. It was a calculated risk, but I knew that by working legally I would be entitled later to a tax refund because of my large family. But I sure didn't want to give my social security number to any other employer. The more people who had it, the more likely it seemed that somebody would find me.

The Andrews brothers didn't ask too many questions, and I didn't offer many details about myself, other than that I had been a soldier in Iraq, and that I had moved with my family from Oklahoma.

I soon had one more reason to keep my employers happy: in the summer of 2004, Brandi was some months pregnant with our fourth child, and decided to quit her job. We didn't have the money to send her to a doctor, and we feared that any contact with the medical world could lead to my arrest. As a result, Brandi had no check-up until the seventh month of her pregnancy. Thankfully, she and the baby seemed healthy, so all we had to do was keep the children quiet as we stayed in hotels and keep working until we could find a way to safety.

Our friend remained in Philadelphia and kept working, and I don't believe we would have survived our long time in hiding without her friendship and support—particularly with babysitting and spotting us money. When we were broke, she never let us do without food, and she never let us down. Twelve dollars an hour seemed like very good money, but it still wasn't enough to keep my family going.

My employers were kind to me. However, they were Republicans, and we argued furiously about the presidential elections in the fall of 2004.

'Of course you like Bush,' I told them. 'You guys are getting richer and richer.'

We argued about Bush, and we argued about the war in Iraq, but didn't tell them about the things I had done or the things I had seen.

Sometimes human kindness comes at the most unexpected moments. Not long after President Bush was re-elected, I told my bosses that my twenty-five-year-old Camaro had broken down so badly that even I couldn't fix it. Rich and Bob Andrews said they had to step out to lunch, and they asked me to mind the shop. An hour or two later, they returned with a gift for me: a 1994 Buick Skylark, complete with new licence plates. It was ten years old, but in better condition than any car I had ever owned before. It must have cost them a good two thousand dollars, and I would have liked to return the favour by staying a long time on the job. I took the gift because we needed it desperately, but I took it with a sense of guilt. It was dawning on me that to have a shot at a decent life, we would have to leave the United States.

Using the internet access provided by hotels, I began to look online for information about war deserters and people who could help me. I had no experience with internet searches, but finally, after typing something like 'war deserter needs help' into Google, I came across details about an American army deserter named Jeremy Hinzman. Apparently, Hinzman had left the United States and was applying for refugee status in Canada. If he was in Canada and hoping to find help, I figured there might be a chance for my family and me.

In October, using the address lotsofkeys@aol.com, I emailed Jeffry House, the Toronto lawyer who was representing Jeremy Hinzman. I didn't give him my name. For all I knew, he could be an army agent posing as a lawyer to catch fugitives like me. I said I was a war deserter and asked if he could help. He gave me the email address and telephone number of a Toronto group called the War Resisters Support Campaign.

I called a woman there by the name of Michelle Robidoux, and described my situation, without giving my name. She promised that her group would help me if I got across the border. At Brandi's urging, I repeated I would be travelling with a wife and four children. Michelle reassured me that they would find a place for our whole family to stay. I didn't call her again for months, and I hoped she wasn't setting a trap for me.

■

Christmas came and went, and we had no money for presents for the boys or ourselves. Thankfully, however, Brandi had been able to get free health care from the State of Pennsylvania for the last part of her pregnancy and her delivery.

When labour began two days after Christmas, our friend stayed with our three boys while I drove Brandi to the hospital. I had always wanted to have a girl, but now I could barely think about it because I was terrified that the army would nab me in the hospital delivery room. While I looked outside the hospital windows for government cars, Brandi had our baby after four hours of labour.

We had a girl and named her Anna. She nearly died on her first day. She had aspirated meconium in the womb and developed pneumonia after she was born. The same day that she came into the world—27 December—Anna had to be rushed to another hospital for emergency care. But she recovered, and we took her back to our hotel three weeks later.

As poor as we were, it seemed a miraculous gift to have a baby daughter. It struck me, as we drove back to the hotel where our friend was camped out again with our boys, that the gift of a daughter might never have been mine if I had returned to fight again in Iraq. Rather than helping to create a new life, I might have ended that of somebody else.

■

It seemed unbelievably risky to leave the United States and enter a foreign country with nothing more to go on than a promise a stranger had made over the phone. But staying in my own country was even more dangerous. If I stayed, eventually something would go wrong and I would get caught. And if I stayed, I was condemning my wife and my children to a never-ending life on the run.

Going to Canada offered the only real chance for me to avoid going to back to Iraq or serving time behind bars. I knew almost nothing about Canada or Canadians. I had heard that they spoke English and French, but I didn't even know the name of Paul Martin, who was prime minister at the time.

We needed some money in case things went terribly wrong for us in the new country, and the only way to do that was to file a tax return in early 2005, knowing that I was likely to get a big refund. It was a risky thing to do, but I had to hope that the IRS and the American army had bigger fish than me to fry, and that even if they did decide to put their heads together and nail me, that it would take them some time.

As soon as I got the necessary forms from my employer, I took my tax return to an H&R Block office in Philadelphia. I had to give an address, so I gave that of the hotel where we had been staying. We then moved into an apartment that our friend had rented so that we could no longer be found at the address on the tax return. The six of us stayed in a one-bedroom apartment. It wasn't comfortable, but we lived better than most Iraqis under American occupation. We had all the water we needed, no bombs were falling through our roof and no soldiers were busting down our door.

In March, I received a federal cheque for about $3000. It was the most money I had ever had in my life, and it would have to be enough for our trip to Canada. I gave our friend the car we had been using, because it wasn't big enough for a family of six. To replace the Buick Skylark, I bought a 1992 Dodge Caravan—with 202,000 miles on the odometer—for $600.

I called Michelle Robidoux one last time at the War Resisters' office in Toronto. She warned us that a border official might ask for details about where we were staying in Canada. In that case, we were to give the name, address and telephone number of a person in Toronto who was a friend of the War Resisters' movement.

Michelle also instructed us to say that we were coming to Toronto to see the musical *Mamma Mia*. And she gave me the name and address of a couple who would let us stay in their home for free. I asked once more if she knew that I was coming with a wife and four children. Yes, Michelle said, that would not be a problem. I told her the day that I would try to enter Canada, and that I would do so at the border at Buffalo.

But I lied.

I did not cross that day, and I did not cross at Buffalo because I felt there was a chance that I was being set up by US Army officials. Two days after I said I was coming, we drove to the border at Niagara Falls, New York, with Brandi at the wheel. My driver's licence had expired, but hers was up to date.

Sucking up the courage to drive to the border of my own country was the hardest thing I had ever done. It would have been easier in some ways to go back to war and serve my time. It would have caused a lot less stress for me to sit in a jail cell. But I didn't want to participate in an unjust war, and didn't believe that it was right that I should become a prisoner in my own country for refusing to act like a criminal in Iraq. The only right choice was to move forward, and I did it with my wife and my children beside me.

I could hardly breathe on the drive to the border. Brandi and I cooked up an insane plan about how, if it looked like officials were going to arrest me, she would try to distract them and give me an opportunity to run away or even jump from a bridge. But in my heart I knew that there was no escape in my own country. This was the moment of truth. I would either get out or I would be arrested. And if I got arrested, there was always the chance that they would arrest Brandi for assisting in my escape. And then what would happen to our children?

I also knew that if I somehow managed to make it across the border with no passports and no up-to-date identification, that I would never again be able to return to my country.

Brandi and I had already lost touch with our families. With the exception of my brother and my mother, most of our relatives saw me as a traitor and a coward. From what I heard,

Brandi's relatives felt that I had ruined her life and turned us all into criminals. We had just said goodbye to our one true friend, who who would finally be returning to her home after over a year away.

We arrived around noon, hoping that the border officials would be busy processing traffic and unlikely to take a close look at us.

'Citizenship?' the border guard asked.

'American,' Brandi said.

'What kind of work do you do?'

'I'm a waitress and my husband is a welder.'

'Where are you heading?'

'Toronto.'

'What's going on there?'

'We're going to visit a friend for the weekend,' Brandi said.

'Why do you have all that stuff along with you?'

'You know what it's like, travelling with kids,' Brandi said.

'Have a nice visit,' he said.

We said goodbye to our country and drove into Canada.

# NINE
## EPILOGUE

My grandfather, Elmer Porter, had a blackout a few months ago. It was the summer of 2006, and his tour of duty as an American soldier in the Korean War had finished more than half a century earlier. He had retired long ago from his job as a mechanic at the Tinker Air Force Base in Oklahoma, and was living quietly on his forty-acre farm. One day, for no particular reason, he thought he was under attack. He thrashed and fought to the limit of his strength, and when he snapped out if it, he discovered that he had trashed his own living room.

A Canadian psychiatrist told me that you never truly emerge from Post-traumatic Stress Disorder, but that you simply learn to live with it.

There are certain things that I avoid these days, such as alcohol and crowds, because I fear they will trigger more of my own blackouts. I know that thousands of American soldiers have abused drugs or committed suicide after returning home from war.

It would be easy to follow in the steps of many in my own family and drown my shame and my sorrows in alcohol. Alcohol, however, could lead to the very problem of suicidal depression that has plagued vets for generations. I won't go down that road.

I have a wife and four children who need me, and they are the single greatest reason why I want to stay alive and to lead a good life. As for the big city, well, I remain an Oklahoma boy at heart, and I like wide-open spaces, so I have fled Toronto and settled in the Canadian prairies.

I am not a man to lead countries or direct armies. I have my high school diploma from Guthrie, Oklahoma, and if I am lucky one day we will move closer to a school where I can learn the trade of welding.

When I was still a soldier in Iraq, I heard that many of the sappers who were discharged from American military service went on to defuse mines in war-torn lands such as the former Yugoslavia. I think of the countless children who have died, or who have had to learn to go on living with missing limbs, because they stepped on a mine—sometimes years after war officially ended in their country.

I think of all the land that can't be trespassed or safely used, because men who passed that way earlier were trying to kill each other. Mines do more than insult people—they also poison their future. In my military training in Missouri and Colorado, I loved the challenge of setting and stripping a mine, and learned to work with nimble fingers under pressure. But I sure wouldn't want to live anywhere near the place where a soldier like me had been busy at work. A lot of ingenuity goes into killing, and it seems to me now a sad waste of money and intelligence. Somebody has to clear minefields in countries where men have stopped fighting, but I am not in any shape to join the brave sappers who have taken on that work.

War took all the fun and the challenge out of guns and bombs for me. Given what I've seen of what guns and bombs do to people, I can't go back to them now and hang onto my sanity. These days my personal and family ambitions are simple, yet hard to obtain. I would like to dream, without nightmares about the people that I traumatised in Iraq. I would like to have a few acres of land and make a steady living as a welder so that my children can grow up decently clothed and properly fed. I want to be a good man to my wife, who gave up her family and her country to support me in my flight from the war in Iraq.

I grew up drinking and fighting and placing beer bottles on my rifle range, and rarely stopped to imagine life outside Oklahoma. I expected to grow old and die in the very place I was born. When I first met Brandi, I told her that I loved Guthrie and never wanted to leave it. I was not a political man. As a child and teenage boy, the most political thought that entered my head were the words of my grandfather, Elmer, who told me that in the United States, the Republican Party stood for the rich and that everyone else should vote for the Democrats.

I'm glad I had Elmer in my life. A lot of men moved in and out with my mother, and I still cringe at memories of her body being flung against the wall of our two-bedroom trailer. They say that you end up doing what the people in your family did. I'm determined that will not be me. No way. My grandfather was the only person I ever knew to tell me that no man had any business beating his wife. I'm glad I had that one good voice in my childhood. His is the one I have chosen to hear.

I like to think that it was my grandfather's voice—the voice of right and wrong—that woke me from the long sleep that I fell into during military training and the first months of war.

There is no excuse for the things that I did in Iraq, or for the beatings I delivered while training with the American army in Missouri. Looking back, I am filled with shame that I beat up other recruits just to please my drill sergeant. I am disgusted to think that I tried to break a man's ribs by swinging away with a soap-filled sock, just because he resisted an order. In the end, the man I beat up was the one with the brains. He had the courage to stand up to an institution that was bent on breaking him and re-casting him as a killer, and it appears that in the end, he managed to get out of the military. That was good for him, and good for Iraq.

My commanders told me that it is army first, God second and family third, but I'll never buy into that way of thinking again. If you have beaten or killed an innocent person, and if there remains a shred of conscience in your heart, you will not avoid anguish by saying that you were only following orders.

We each have to find what we believe to be the right way to live. When we prosecute an unjust war, or commit immoral acts in any war at all, the first victims are the people unfortunate enough to fall into our hands. The next victims are ourselves. We damage ourselves each time we violate our own true beliefs, and the wrongs we commit weigh on our shoulders to the grave.

I cannot say exactly what would have happened if I had refused to blow apart the homes of Iraqis; if I had refused to send every male over five feet in height to American detention centres. I imagine that I would have been humiliated and punished by my superiors. I may have been beaten. Perhaps they would have sent me home to prison or disgrace. But if every single soldier in the American army had refused to blow off the doors of houses in the residential streets of Iraq, I will bet you that the generals and colonels and captains who commanded us—and our president and commander-in-chief, George W. Bush—would not have volunteered for the job.

I am ashamed of what I did in Iraq, and of all the ways that innocent civilians suffered or died at our hands. The fact that I was only following orders does not lessen my discomfort or ease my nightmares. After I came across the four decapitated heads by the side of the road in Ramadi, and saw soldiers in my own army kicking these heads for their own amusement, I began to dream of the incident and of the rolling heads— even though I had arrived after the murder. The very fact that I saw it and was part of the machine that committed the act weighed on my soul and weighs on it still.

I believe that some people will say that Americans faced a nasty, unconventional war in Iraq, and that we had no choice but to take the war to our enemy in unconventional ways.

My feeling is that we lacked the information, the skill and the experience to find our true enemies in Iraq. We liked to think of the Iraqi fighters as inhuman and as stupid, but the fact of the matter is that they outfoxed the American military wherever I went. They threw mortars and grenades our way, and we never even saw them running away. My fellow combatants and I never once put an armed enemy in our gunsights. They were on the run and gone while we were still diving for cover against flying shrapnel. We fought back by lashing out at civilians who had no means to defend themselves. It was in the only way we could fight back—but it was wrong.

I don't think that senior American military commanders made soldiers raid thousands of civilian houses because they truly believed that we would nab terrorists or find weapons of mass destruction. I think they did it to punish and intimidate the Iraqi people.

In the eyes of the American military, Iraqis were not people at all—they were 'terrorists', 'suicide bombers', 'sand niggers', 'rag heads'. We had to think of them as less than human in order to keep doing the things that we did. We were taught to think of Iraqis in degrading ways during military training, and those attitudes crossed the oceans with us when we flew into battle.

The Geneva Conventions are international agreements— which the United States and almost all other nations have signed—that aim to limit the barbarity of war by protecting civilians and prisoners of war. Basically, they set out the dos and don'ts of war. The most significant don'ts are not hard to imagine: soldiers are not to steal from, beat, torture, rape or kill civilians or prisoners of war. I won't go on and on about all of the Geneva Conventions that we violated in Iraq, but I do want to quote one in particular:

> Parties to the conflict shall at all times distinguish between the civilian population and combatants and between civilian objects and military objectives and accordingly shall direct their operations only against military objectives.

I would not have deserted my army, left my country or chosen to speak out against the war in Iraq if American soldiers in my company had limited themselves to fighting enemy combatants.

I left the war because the American army made no distinction between civilians and combatants. We were taught to see all Iraqis as enemies, and we were encouraged to keep thinking this way from the first day that my 43rd Combat Engineer Company pulled into the city of Ramadi.

I hold my army in judgment for the repeated abuses of Iraqi civilians, but I hold myself in judgment too.

When Nazi war criminals were brought to justice at the Nuremburg trials, an important principle was established: claiming that one is just following the orders of a superior does not relieve oneself from the responsibilities of international law, provided that a moral choice was possible.

I had not read about the Geneva Conventions or the Nuremburg trials before setting foot in Iraq. But all I had to do was think of the teachings of my own grandfather at home to know that I had no business abusing civilians in another country.

I am responsible for the things that I did. And my commanders were even more responsible for putting us there and ordering us to do the things we did. It was bad enough that nobody was monitoring our behaviour in Iraq or holding us accountable for it. But the situation was made worse because we had tacit approval from our commanders to shoot first and ask questions later.

If a soldier beat up or shot somebody, all he had to say—if he said anything at all—was that he felt threatened. As a result, our behaviour remained unchecked. That's why it was possible for American soldiers to decapitate Iraqis by means of machine-gun fire and kick about their heads as objects of play.

In Iraq, I did not witness an equivalent of the 1968 massacre of hundreds of unarmed Vietnamese citizens by Americans in the hamlet of My Lai. Instead, I saw a steady stream of abuse and individual killing—a punch here, a shot there. Collectively, however, these incidents added up. If the crimes committed against civilians by members of my 43rd Combat Engineer Company were added to all the others carried out by other American soldiers in Iraq, I suspect that the total number of victims would shock and astonish Americans just as profoundly as the discovery of the My Lai massacre.

Sometimes I wonder how the world might change if—with my own eyes and perhaps with a camera on my shoulder—I had witnessed every civilian beating and murder that American soldiers have carried out in Iraq. I wonder what would happen if every atrocity were compressed into the same day and the same city, still with my eyes watching and my camera ready. Then, I suspect, Americans would rise up with the same sort of protests that brought an end to the Vietnam War. Alone, I cannot paint such a picture. But I know what I have seen. And I believe it is part of a much wider picture. I shudder to imagine the thousands upon thousands of Iraqi families who this very day are struggling still with the loss of a loved one who died, completely innocent, at American hands.

When American soldiers beat up, stole from and killed Iraqi civilians during my six and a half months at war, I saw them do so with complete impunity. We were far more than soldiers fighting enemy insurgents. To the civilians of Iraq, we became police officers, prosecutors, jailors and executioners.

We claimed to be bringing democracy and order to the people of Iraq, but all we brought was hate and destruction. The only thing we gave to the Iraqi people was a reason to despise us—and perhaps to want to kill us—for generations to come.

In my last months there, I met soldiers who felt the same way that I did. For the most part, though, we kept our mouths shut. We lived in a military culture that had already taught us that although we could get away with beating or even killing Iraqi civilians, punishment would be swift and harsh if we opposed our commanders. By remaining silent, we made it possible for the abuses to continue.

I do not know what all of the other companies of the American Forces were doing while I was busy with the 43rd Combat Engineer Company. But since coming to Canada, I have read accounts of convictions against members of my 3rd Armored Cavalry regiment for the abuse of Iraqi civilians and the torture and murder of at least one prisoner of war. I never met the people who have been convicted, and I did not know of them when I was at war. Sadly, it does not surprise me that they belonged to the 3rd Armored Cavalry Regiment.

On 26 November 2003—just two weeks after I left Iraq— an Iraqi major general by the name of Abed Hamed

Mowhoush died while being interrogated and tortured by members of the 3rd Armored Cavalry Regiment. Mowhoush had surrendered to American soldiers in my regiment in a vain attempt to obtain the release of two of his sons who had been captured earlier. As a choking technique, water was poured down his throat. He was also stuffed head-first into a sleeping bag and wrapped in electrical cord during one interrogation. Subsequently, a US military court convicted Chief Warrant Officer Lewis Welshofer—also from Fort Carson—of negligent homicide in Mowhoush's death. Welshofer's punishment was a reprimand and a $6000 fine. I wonder what punishment a court would have meted out if the victim had been American citizen.

And a Captain Shawn Martin—who, like Welshofer, was part of the 3rd ACR—was charged on accusations that he had used a pistol, his fists and a baseball bat that he called his 'Iraqi beater' to threaten and abuse civilians and his own troops in an Iraqi town by the name of Rutbah. Martin was eventually convicted of three counts of assault against Iraqi civilians. His lawyer claimed that Martin was a good soldier who was authorised to use tough techniques. Martin's punishment: a $12,000 fine and forty-five days behind bars.

After I left Iraq and came to Canada, it came to light that American soldiers had been humiliating and abusing prisoners at the Abu Ghraib prison south of Baghdad. Two soldiers—neither of them members of my 3rd ACR—were jailed for taking photographs of prisoners in forced poses. As mentioned earlier, I had no idea where our troops sent all the men and the boys that were detained in house raids. Every single male over five feet tall was zipcuffed, head-bagged and tossed onto the back of the five-ton truck duti-fully waiting outside each house that we raided, ransacked and plundered.

I still shake my head in shame and wonderment when I think of the Iraqi man who—as he was being seized by my squad mates—had the guts to shout out in anger on seeing me stuff his American bills into my pants.

'Why are you taking that money? It's not yours.'

I kept the money, and for a good while I held the attitude that Iraqis had no rights in their own country. It was an attitude I had picked up from my commanders, and it took me an embarrassingly long period of time before I began to question and then reject it.

When I fled to Canada, I was required to make a deposition to the Canadian Immigration and Refugee Board, stating why I was seeking official refugee status. In this book, I have addressed all the facts set out in that deposition, and have written for the first time about a number of other incidents that I also witnessed in Iraq. However, there are two details in the deposition that I wish to correct, for the record.

The first has to do with the killing of a child in al-Habbaniyah shortly after my platoon raided a home inhab-ited by two disabled men. The deposition says that the victim was a boy. That is an error. The child was a girl. I am not sure how it came to be recorded incorrectly in the deposition, but

I remember all too well that young girl in her school uniform, and I always will.

The second detail relates to the number of houses my platoon mates and I raided in Iraq. The deposition says that I conducted about 75 raids. At the time that I prepared the deposition, I was anxious to avoid any possibility of over-stating the number of raids. However, after making that first statement, I have had many more months to reflect on the matter and to do a tally of our raids. I now realise that two hundred raids is a far more accurate figure, and I believe that this estimate is still conservative.

If we detained an average of one male per home—and that would be a conservative estimate—that means that the men in my squad alone sent two hundred men into detention centres and prisons. I can only imagine that some of them ended up at Abu Ghraib.

Some people will say that the terrible things that I have described here were exceptions to the rule. That might be comforting, but it would be naïve. I saw fundamental viola-tions of basic human rights every day or two for six months in Iraq, and since I never saw one soldier or officer criticised or disciplined for carrying out such violations, I tend to fear the opposite.

And what I saw was only the tip of the iceberg in Iraq. I know that on two occasions that I did encounter other military companies, I came across the murder of Iraqis that I believed to be civilians. I am thinking of members of the 82nd Airborne Division who shot and killed twelve civilians in

Fallujah. And I am thinking of the members of the Florida National Guard who shot up four Iraqis so mercilessly in Ramadi that they ended up decapitating them and playing with the heads. When I came upon him and his buddies as they stood close to the heads. By a fluke of timing, I caught one American soldier in a moment of complete honesty. 'We fucking lost it, we just fucking lost it!' He said it when the heads had just been severed and the blood was still fresh. He said it before he knew enough to shut his mouth. And as far as I could tell, he was speaking the ugly truth.

In our military training and in our daily experiences at war, American soldiers were taught to show no regard for the lives of Iraqis—not even for civilians. This will go on until one of two things happen: the people of America no longer tolerate it, or the people of Iraq find their own ways to strike back at us.

In my opinion, the September 11 attacks on the United States were cowardly and despicable crimes. On that day, the terrorists had no right or reason to take the lives of American civilians. But I fear that our own behaviour in Iraq has invited more of the same. The young Iraqis who survive our raids, abuse and detention have all the motivation they need to seek revenge. I am not looking forward to the day that they get organised. Whenever I remember shouting, together with 300 military trainees in Missouri, 'Kill the sand niggers!' while we stabbed and slashed at straw dummies with our bayonets, I hope that the Iraqis who survive our war prove to be more civilised than we were.

■

When I was in high school, I would have scoffed if one of my friends had predicted that I would one day become an anti-war activist. If somebody had suggested that newspapers, magazines and documentary films in North America, Europe and Japan would be examining my role in the war in Iraq and talking about why I had run from it, I would have thought that they were out of their mind.

I grew up a patriot, I entered the American army as a patriot, and I commenced duties in Iraq—raiding homes, patrolling streets and checking cars—as a patriot. I hated to read and write as a child, but if somebody had forced me to predict—maybe in my school yearbook—what would happen in my future, I would have written that I would have a family, believe in my country and my government, and become a working man in Guthrie, Oklahoma.

Going to war in Iraq and then going AWOL—first in my own country and then fleeing to Canada—forced me to give up many things. I had to give up my unexamined belief that my country and my army were a force for good in the world. I had to give up my assumptions that leaders of my own country would speak the truth when they spoke to me. I learned the hard way that it was not true that I could sign up for the military and choose to become a bridge builder in the continental United States. The way the military reeled in the other recruits and me—many black and Latino, and all poor—I now call the poverty draft.

It was not true that Saddam Hussein possessed weapons of

mass destruction. And it was not true that every man, woman and child in Iraq was an evil terrorist who deserved American hatred, bombs and occupation. All I had to do was look in the eyes of a seven-year-old girl who ran to me to ask for my rations, day after day until she was shot dead, to know that the people we intimidated, beat, detained and killed were human beings with the same hungry stomachs as my American-born children.

When I finally abandoned my country and entered Canada, I had to leave behind a number of attitudes that I barely knew I had. My grandfather—the same one who passed on the good values that helped me find my own conscience in Iraq—was not a perfect man. He was an out and out racist, and he believed that Asian peoples were the enemies of Americans. When Brandi, the children and I crossed the border at Niagara Falls, New York, we drove to Toronto and stayed for six months—at no charge—in the home of Winnie and Eugene Ng, two Asian Canadians. I hadn't known many gentle care-givers in my early years in Oklahoma. In a way, Winnie and Eugene became caring parents to Brandi and me. Our own boys call them 'Grandma Winnie' and 'Grandpa Eugene'.

All I had to do was spend an hour at the table of Winnie and Eugene to realise how sadly mistaken my grandfather had been.

Grandfather Elmer had fought in Korea and I imagine that he had found it necessary to demonise and hate the people he fought. But I don't have to keep my grandfather's demons alive. And I don't have to nourish the demons that I was taught in my own training in the American army.

Because I fought an unconventional war in Iraq, and because that war brought me into close contact with ordinary civilians who were struggling to survive—in the very ways that Americans would be struggling to survive, if the tables were turned—I was able to awaken slowly to the humanity of the very people I was taught to despise. Coming to Toronto and staying with Winnie and Eugene moved me along the same path. It showed me how easy it was to put my own grandfather's demons to sleep. That is one less demon for me to pass onto my children.

If every American soldier set aside his or her M-249 automatic rifle and sat down to dinner with an Iraqi family, I believe that the house raids the next day would be less brutal. If the dinners continued, perhaps the raids would come to an end. I believe that even the most patriotic soldiers in my company would hesitate to beat up, zipcuff and arrest a sixteen-year-old boy if they had discovered that the teenager liked falafels and mint tea and studied trigonometry in the hope that one day, if the universities open up again, he could learn from the brightest minds still alive in his country.

The War Resisters Support Campaign is a Toronto-based group with volunteers around the country. They help out the thirty or so deserters who, like me, have applied for refugee status in Canada. They provided food for my family during our first months there and I did my best to pay them back by speaking at public events about my experiences in Iraq.

I will never forget the first time I was asked to speak in

public. It was at a meeting of the Canadian Labour Congress, just a month or so after we arrived in Toronto. I was so terrified that I could barely open my mouth. Eventually, I grew into public speaking. In the summer of 2005, Brandi, the children and I drove from Toronto to the Pacific Coast and back, stopping for me to give talks in some twenty towns and cities along the way. I spoke in churches, mosques, libraries and community halls. I met with journalists everywhere I went. All I wanted to do was tell people what I had seen and done, and why I had chosen to desert the American army in Iraq.

I especially liked speaking in mosques. I was worried at first that I might be received with hatred and accusations. But each time I have been received warmly and encouraged to speak about my experiences at war and why I deserted the army. I live with the things that I did in Iraq a little easier when I speak to Muslims in Canada. I tell them that I am sorry about what I did to their brothers and sisters, and that I hope they can find it in their hearts to forgive me. Prospects for peace do not look good in the world, but I believe that individual citizens can make a difference. For my part, I speak to as many people as I can about the things that I did and saw in Iraq. I am grateful to break bread with Muslims when they invite me to meet with them.

As this book goes to press, Americans still occupy Iraq and Canadians have joined aggressive military action in Afghanistan. I have not been to Afghanistan, and I do not know exactly what Canadian, American and other international troops are doing to the civilians of that country. The truth will come out one of these days, and I hope we do not discover that soldiers in Afghanistan have been carrying out the same litany of abuses that I helped deliver in Iraq.

Although some Canadians have threatened me—one man in British Columbia even threatened to put me in a boat and drag me across to the American border—most people in this new country have treated me well. It remains to be seen whether the government of Canada will allow me to stay. I have argued before to the Canadian Immigration and Refugee Board that other war deserters and myself should be allowed to stay. I have argued that it would be wrong for Canada to force me to return to a country that repeatedly ordered me to abuse Iraqi civilians. I don't think it's right that I should serve jail time in the United States or be sent back to do more of the same in Iraq.

Some thirty years ago, under the leadership of the late Pierre Trudeau, the Canadian government welcomed draft dodgers from the Vietnam War. The current Canadian government, led by Prime Minister Stephen Harper, has not looked favourably on refugee claims made by recent deserters of the American army. My case is unusual because I am the first deserter in Canada to argue that I went AWOL after being ordered to take part in a steady stream of human rights violations in Iraq. Still, I am not optimistic about my future, and any day now, I could be told to pack my bags and leave. Any day now, my family's life could be completely torn apart.

If I have any choice in the matter, I will not return to the

United States. I have lost my country, and it has lost me. I would only reconsider this position if the United States jailed President George W. Bush and all the senior military officials responsible for sending our abusive army into Iraq.

I would be willing to sit in a jail cell with the president. But I would not use my hands on him. Much as I think the man deserves a licking, I'm through with physical abuse—in Oklahoma, in American boot camps, in Iraq and everywhere else in the world. If I were alone in a jail cell with President Bush, I would use words and try to talk some sense into his head.

If I had the chance to have a man-to-man talk with the President of the United States, I would tell him to take a look at the laws and the Constitution of his own country. He needs to know that during the time I served in the war in Iraq, soldiers and officers of the American forces violated the very values that we claim to uphold in our own nation. If the president wishes to know exactly what values I am talking about, I would direct him to some of the first words of the American Declaration of Independence of 1776:

> We hold these truths to be self-evident, that all men are created equal, that they are endowed by their Creator with certain unalienable Rights, that among these are Life, Liberty and the pursuit of Happiness.

Although I would love to sit down with the president, I would like even more to have half an hour with every young American who is thinking of signing up for the poverty draft. As poor and as desperate as my young family was when I drove to the recruiting centre in Oklahoma in March of 2002, I would *never* have signed up if I knew that I would be blasting into Iraqis' houses, terrorising women and children and detaining every man we could find—and all that, for $1200 a month as a private first class. Somehow, somewhere, I would have found a job and a way to survive. I would never have gone to war for my country, if I had known what my country was doing at war in Iraq.

Young people need to know that they don't have to live with the moral anguish of fighting an immoral war. It is not true that one's first obligation is to the military, and then to God, and then to family. One's first obligation is to the moral truth buried deep inside our own souls. Every single person knows what is right and wrong. And we have a duty to live up to it, regardless of what our leaders say.

When I came home from Iraq, I was a complete wreck. I had so many nightmares that I had to get prescription pills to help stave off the dreams. I had blackouts. I would cry one moment, and scream the next. I was so paranoid that the simple act of standing in line in a grocery store seemed fraught with peril: somebody, surely, would pull out a gun or rip the pin from a grenade. Every day, I thought of the civilians I had seen arrested, beaten or killed in Iraq. I could not focus. I could not sit still with a child on my lap. I could not deal with the sound of my own children crying, laughing and calling out for my love. My own son Zack grabbed onto me for dear life in an effort to prevent me from disappearing back into 'Sergeant World', but I barely knew how to respond to his love, or give it back to him.

I was a shell of the man who had left the United States just seven months earlier, and I intend always to remember that my wife Brandi loved me and encouraged me and stuck with me even when it meant that we all had to go into a long period of hiding, insecurity and poverty. I paid a price for participating in hurting the people of Iraq. And I wasn't the only one.

When I came home, I told Brandi that I had seen innocent people die in Iraq. For the longest time, that was all she knew. But because she loved me, that was all she needed to hear. In fact, she did not want to hear any details. Taking care of three young boys and me and little Anna who was soon growing in her womb, Brandi did not feel that she had the strength to hear about everything I had seen and done.

Apart from that one time in Philadelphia, when I got drunk and began to shout about the young girl killed outside the hospital in Ramadi, I have never spoken to her about all the intimate details given in this book. She read the information form I gave the Canadian immigration authorities, when I applied for refugee status. And when she put it down, she said she would never have read it in the first place if she had known what she would find.

We both carry emotional wounds as a result of the war in Iraq, and I imagine that thousands of other Americans who served in Iraq have also brought their own personal nightmares back home. Their families too will be suffering.

Ordinary Iraqis have paid very dearly for this war, and ordinary Americans are paying for it too with their lives and with their souls.

I have never been a man to run from a challenge, and I have never fled from danger or abandoned vulnerable people. I am neither a coward nor a traitor. When I was still being recruited in Oklahoma City in 2002, I had to sign a paper to the effect that I had read and understood a warning from the military: 'Desertion in the time of war means death by a firing squad.' That just about sums it up.

We could do whatever we wanted to Iraqis. But if we ran from duty, there would be hell to pay. I will never apologise for deserting the American army. I deserted an injustice and leaving was the only right thing to do. I owe one apology and one apology only, and that is to the people of Iraq.

# ACKNOWLEDGMENTS

We wish to acknowledge the close collaboration that led to the writing of this book, and to thank the people who helped us.

After hearing Joshua Key speak on CBC radio in the spring of 2006, the Canadian literary agent Denise Bukowski contacted him and asked if he would like to write a book about his experiences as an American soldier in Iraq. In April 2006, Joshua Key and Lawrence Hill began to work together. The project began with a series of in-depth interviews conducted in British Columbia, the Canadian Prairies and the Toronto area. Between these intensive sessions, the two were in touch regularly by telephone and email while Lawrence sifted through hundreds of pages of notes and dozens of taped interviews and began to write Josh's story. As the book took shape, Joshua reviewed every line many times to ensure that it accurately reflected his experiences, observations and beliefs. Of the numerous incidents during his service in Iraq, he was extremely careful to recount only what he saw and experienced himself.

Both authors are grateful to their literary agent, Denise Bukowski, for the enthusiasm with which she brought this book to the attention of publishers in numerous countries. We offer special thanks to Morgan Entrekin and Amy Hundley at Atlantic Monthly Press in New York and to Lynn Henry at House of Anansi Press in Toronto, for their commitment and courage in standing behind this book and bringing it to market.

Joshua Key and Lawrence Hill

■

I thank my mother, Judy Porter and brother, Tyler Barker for believing in me during and especially after my service with the American Army in Iraq. I also want to thank Michelle Robidoux and her colleagues at the War Resisters Support Campaign in Toronto, my lawyer Jeffry House, and Winnie and Eugene Ng, Neil and Ruth Loomis, Al and Marjorie Stewart, Lynn Wytenbroek, and Elaine for their generous support. Many other people across the United States and Canada showed kindness to my family and me in times of need, and I thank all of them too.

Joshua Key

■

It has been an honour to work with Joshua Key and to write his story. I thank Joshua and Brandi for the trust they placed in me during our many conversations. As well, I wish to thank my wife, Miranda Hill, for her unwavering support and encouragement.

Lawrence Hill